2016   4   Keip

6/17   3/18

THE FIRST
NAZI

THE FIRST
NAZI

Erich Ludendorff,
The Man Who Made
Hitler Possible

WILL BROWNELL, PH.D.

and

DENISE DRACE-BROWNELL, JD, MPH

WITH ALEXANDER ROVT, PH.D.

Duckworth Overlook

First published in the UK in 2016 by

Duckworth Overlook

LONDON
30 Calvin Street, London E1 6NW
T: 020 7490 7300
E: info@duckworth-publishers.co.uk
www.ducknet.co.uk
For bulk and special sales please contact sales@duckworth-publishers.co.uk, or write
to us at the above address.

First published in the United States by Counterpoint in 2016.

ISBN 978-0-7156-5104-9

10 9 8 7 6 5 4 3 2 1

A catalogue record for this book is available from the British Library.

Interior design by Megan Jones Design

Printed and bound in Great Britain

CONTENTS

INTRODUCTION
The Death of an Assassin

AN AMAZING FUNERAL took place in Germany in December 1937, just before the beginning of the Second World War. At that time General Erich Ludendorff was laid to rest, with Hitler in attendance, in a celebration of Nazi optimism.

The honors were many. *Life* magazine declared that Ludendorff was magnificent, and their headline proclaimed, "Germany Buries the Greatest General of the [First World] War." It was a stupefying statement, declaring this man more remarkable than General Pershing of the US Army; General Foch, the supreme commander of Allied forces in the West; Winston Churchill, the rising young leader in London; General Alexei Brusilov in Moscow; and anyone else of stature. The journal said that Ludendorff was "the ablest general developed by the World War" and "the military peer of Robert E. Lee."

The article explained that Ludendorff was the brains of the German Army; the right-hand of Hindenburg, who led that army; and the supreme strategist of Germany of the time. He had mauled whole armies from Russia, Romania, France, Britain, and Italy. So great was the prestige of Ludendorff and his friend Hindenburg that, the article noted, "Even the Kaiser took orders from them."

The magazine offered some criticisms, though. It claimed that Ludendorff fell apart in defeat when his army died in 1918. And it added that when Germany lost that world war, Ludendorff scurried off like a frightened man, wearing a wig and blue glasses for a disguise, to neutral Sweden. Finally the article reported that Ludendorff was seen as a tad paranoid and that he saw conspiracies everywhere, by the Masons and Jesuits, Catholics and Jews, all of whom he blamed for causing Germany's woes. It also noted that after the First World War, Ludendorff "marched beside Hitler."

But that was all that was negative. Generally the article was positive, with strong praise about Ludendorff's being "the greatest general of the war" and about how he received "a funeral worthy of his place in history." The funeral organizers put Ludendorff's sixty medals on display and brought out a huge military band, which played the German war song "The Good Comrade." It was thunderously impressive.

The only surprise for anyone viewing the photos that accompanied the *Life* magazine article might have been that Ludendorff's coffin was bedecked with the battle flag of the Kaiser and not the swastika of Hitler's new Germany. Some might have guessed that the two had a falling out, but few likely noted the difference. Indeed, it hardly seemed significant at that time.

Amidst all the praise, *Life* did not mention that Ludendorff invented the murderous slander that the Jews had made Germany lose the war, or that in revenge he wanted to gas the Jews the same way that German soldiers had died on the fields of battle—by poison gas. Also, no one noted that Ludendorff had extended Germany's agony in the First World War by two excruciating years, or that he had blocked a compromise peace halfway through that war that could have saved Germany's soul. Nearly no one knew that this man had arranged for Lenin to travel to Russia in a sealed train, like a deadly germ, to infect that nation with a ferocious Communist revolution that would destroy its chances for democracy for a long time to come.

The article did not hint that Ludendorff had launched the "Ludendorff Offensives" against the Allies in 1918, which cost Germany more than 900,000 men, and indeed the war. Nor did the article indicate that Ludendorff, after he lost the war, helped launch the Nazi Party, initiated a powerful propaganda campaign to dismember the new German government, and then worked with his new friend Hitler to map the road to revenge. Remarkably, the article gave no hint that this man had spent the last two decades urging Germans to wage a new war, a war of revenge, to realize all the mad dreams he had failed to achieve in the last great slaughter.

Why did no one sense that this man was sponsoring a savage new age? Why did no one see that this man was pushing Germany toward a gigantic new barbarism, a second world war? Why did no one suggest that his early support of Hitler in the 1920s was vital in helping that madman on his road to power, or that this support aided Hitler to murder so many millions?

Everyone understood that Ludendorff was brilliant in tactics, but few pointed out that he was also a genius when it came to blaming others for his errors. That he could lose the First World War and then blame the Jews for his loss shows this. But how did he do this with no evidence to support the slander?

General Erich Ludendorff may have been one of the two or three most destructive men of the twentieth century. How he accomplished this without being remembered as the assassin that he was, is a staggering story.

This is the story we wish to tell today.

We also wish it understood that we want this book to become accessible history for the public at large, a new kind of serious historical biography.

CHAPTER 1
Ludendorff Begins His War

WORLD WAR I began in a fit of absentmindedness. A mere archduke of Austria and his wife were visiting a minor city called Sarajevo, the capital of Bosnia, on June 28, 1914. A patriotic student named Gavrilo Princip, who wanted the Austrian province to secede and join with Russia, shot the archduke in the chest and, accidently, shot his wife too. The archduke was rushed to the hospital, but the doctor could not unbutton his tunic. He did not know that the elegant archduke was sewn into that tunic every morning, in an effort to look trim. Precious seconds were lost as the doctor tried to get the tunic open to stop the bleeding. Swiftly the well-dressed archduke bled to death.

Furious, Austria demanded satisfaction from Serbia and made brutal ultimatums. Outraged, the German Kaiser, Wilhelm II, backed his Austrian allies. Emboldened, the Austrians declared war on Serbia, whom Russia supported. Russia declared war on Austria in a rage, and Germany then declared war on Russia, equally raging. Russia's ally France then declared war on Germany. England tried to stay out of the fray, and in several respects there were rationales to keep England out. But there were major elements that seemed to force England to participate. For years British statesmen had concluded that it was vital to their interests that no one power become supreme on the continent. This alone seemed to force England to go against Germany. Second, the British had signed a treaty in 1839 pledging that they would help Belgium in just such circumstances as these. And third, the new German Navy, while inferior to the Royal Navy of England, was nonetheless seen as a major threat to Britain's sea power. These three reasons, no one of which was vital, were decisive in sum. And in just a few days the awesome power of imperial Britain entered the conflict, with staggering consequences. In weeks Europe was at war.

Germany was outnumbered five to one. And from the onset it was in a two-front war, with Russia to the east and France to the west. Generally, a two-front war is a death sentence. But the German generals were not worried. A brilliant field marshal named Alfred von Schlieffen had put together a deployment strategy, the so-called Schlieffen Plan, which many Germans felt was a guarantee of victory.

After studying the military tactics of Hannibal, that great general of antiquity, the count believed that one smaller power could overwhelm greater powers by attacking both sides of an invading enemy, the way Hannibal did at Cannae in the third century before Christ. Schlieffen decided that he could send great armies west into France and Belgium, destroy those nations in four weeks, and then turn around and send the same German armies into Russia and destroy that nation in four months.

If this plan had worked the Germans would have seized Europe in record time. It seemed perfect if one accepted its underlying assumptions. But it assumed that one could take a battle plan from the third century before Christ, one that applied to 30,000 men, and apply it in the twentieth century, with a modern army in the millions. Worse, it assumed that this enormous number of troops could perform on a tight timetable at top speed, win the war in the West, then turn around swiftly and do the same in the East. It also assumed that the small Belgian Army would not have the courage to defend its homeland. Finally it presumed that patriotic Belgians could not obstruct passage by dynamiting the limited roads and bridges of their country.

Such were the proud assumptions of Germans at the beginning of their war, and they were so erroneous that modern historians view the plan as flawed from the beginning. Where to begin with the list of dissenters? Major General David T. Zabecki, the American editor of the four-volume encyclopedia *Germany at War*, is one. German historians Hans Ehlert, Michael Epkenhans, and Gerhard Gross at the Bundeswehr Center for [German] Military History in Potsdam, Germany, are three more.

Perhaps the finest critic of this plan was Gerhard Ritter. Ritter was a German soldier in World War I, and he later became a fine military historian for thirty-one years at the University of Freiburg. He had no patience with those who upheld the brilliance of Schlieffen. In a devastating book titled *The Schlieffen Plan: Critique of a Myth*, he made what might be the best analysis of the plan: "Going from clue to clue, it becomes evident that the secret of the Schlieffen Plan, and the basis of Schlieffen's formula for a quick victory, amounted to little more than a gambler's belief in the virtuosity of sheer audacity. Its magic is a myth. As a strategic concept it proved a snare and delusion for the executants, with fatal consequences that were . . . inherently probable from the outset. . . . It assumed a perfection that could not be achieved, and had no provision for the unexpected."

The Germans assumed that the Belgians would be easy to conquer. But once their nation was invaded, the Belgians fought hard. Caesar, who had fought all the tribes of Gaul and Belgium, would not have been surprised. Said he: "Of all these, most noble are the Belgians." Caesar knew. The moment the Germans invaded, Belgian resistance exploded. They ruined their bridges and railroads, slowing down the Germans' advance badly. The Belgians could come to the front by rail from the west, where the railroads were still intact. But the Germans had to come on foot through ravaged territory to the east, where the rails had been ruined by patriots and guerrillas. Meanwhile snipers shot at the Germans from haystacks, trees, and ravines. Schoolboys, priests, nuns, teachers, and police did what they could—people found pitchforks, scythes, pistols, and axes to stop any invaders. Enraged, the Germans fumed that this self-defense was illegal (as if their invasion were not?), and they shot 4,000 Belgian hostages in just the first two months of the war. They lashed out blindly, burned whole towns, and deported thousands of men as forced laborers.

A German-born Belgian princess, Princess Elizabeth, came to despise her fellow Germans so much that she coined a phrase about this behavior that would be repeated by Churchill and many other leaders over the years, in one context and another. Said she: "Between me and them there has descended an Iron Curtain, which nothing can remove."

Everything seemed to conspire to slow down the German advance, especially in the city of Liege. The Belgians there possessed huge forts with walls thirteen feet thick, and here they resisted hard. And it was at this time that an unknown German general named Erich Ludendorff brought in new heavy artillery, the most effective cannon the world had known. One such cannon named Big Bertha was a seventy-five-ton monster pulled by hundreds of horses and served by a crew of 280 soldiers. This giant made the earth quake as it moved down a highway. Its shells weighed more than a ton and hit targets eight miles distant.

Ludendorff fired and fired, smashing the magnificent forts that had never been designed for such concussions. Yet still the Belgians resisted. Whole sectors of the forts imploded, the heat rose up, and the ventilation systems broke down, but nothing seemed to dishearten these men. Only when a lucky shell detonated the gunpowder room in the main fortress, slaughtering some of the best men in the headquarters, did Belgian resistance break.

The Germans celebrated their tardy victory even though the delay upset their invasion plan. Ludendorff, previously unknown, became the hero of the hour. They gave him a medal known as the Blue Max, the highest honor his army could confer. It seemed as if Germany were winning the world.

But it was losing the world instead. The German chief of staff, Helmuth von Moltke, knew the real story. He understood that Germany's master plan was being ruined and that the war was being lost in these slow victories. And then came the news that the Russians were advancing ahead of schedule.

Russia had an alliance with France—it was the price the Russians paid to get the gigantic loans they needed to develop Siberia and build the great Trans-Siberian Railway. And now the Russians were honoring this alliance and advancing in the East, far earlier than expected, into the swamps of Prussia, threatening the Germans' plans in that sector. On August 20, 1914, at a town called Gumbinnen, the Germans tried to blunt the Russian advance.

But for once the Russians had superb heavy artillery, and it all was arranged in perfect fields of fire. They even had reserves of shells, to launch thundering assaults.

According to the Schlieffen Plan this was not supposed to happen. The Germans had seen the Russians as incompetent because they had performed so poorly in their previous war, fought against Japan in 1905. Russians were supposed to be slow. Yet now they fired with accuracy and heavy artillery, and they obliterated a German army and captured 6,000 prisoners. Maximilian von Prittwitz, the German commander in East Prussia, whose nickname was Fatty, cabled Berlin for permission to retreat to the west of the Vistula River. This craven retreat would have given most of eastern Prussia to Russia.

Incredible rumors of Russian atrocities, mostly tales of rape and pillage, were now sweeping Germany. Many German generals had ancestral homes in the Prussian region of Germany, and they were anxious to defend these estates. "What good does it do if we take Paris or Brussels," men asked, "if the Cossacks take Berlin?"

The high command became apoplectic at von Prittwitz's suggestion of a retreat and sacked him on the spot. This was the first time a German general had been removed in battle. The high command then instructed their new hero, Ludendorff, to move east and take command along with another general, Paul Hindenburg, whom they had convinced to come out of retirement. This move was unprecedented. Ludendorff, who did not even have an aristocratic "von" to his name, was now one of just two German officers directing their government's main efforts in this great and terrible war. Thus began the most important military partnership in the First World War, a partnership that would have huge victories but would ultimately lose everything in a four-year whirlwind of up-heaval and destruction.

Ludendorff and Hindenburg began their partnership on a de-serted railway platform in eastern Germany. According to all re-ports, Ludendorff came out of his railway car onto the platform and saluted smartly. The old general, Hindenburg, returned the sa-lute in a ponderous way. Strangely, the old general was wearing the old German uniform that they no longer issued. The young officer Ludendorff was all energy, full of action, and wearing the new grey field uniform, whose color was inspired by the grey of old Greek statues. The older officer took it all in.

The military situation was grim. The German plan for victory was breaking down in the East and the West at the same time. And to make matters worse, the German military had no backup plan. The battle plan they were using was like a parachute: It had to work.

In his pocket Ludendorff carried a cautious message from Helmuth von Moltke, chief of the German General Staff: "A new and difficult task is entrusted to you. . . . I know of no other man in whom I have such absolute trust. You may yet be able to save the situation in the East. . . . Of course you will not be made respon-sible for what has already happened, but with your energy, you can prevent the worst from happening." And from Ludendorff's quartermaster, there was another reassuring note: "Your task is a difficult one but you are equal to it."

The two generals sized each other up. Hindenburg was easily recognizable as a Junker officer of the old style, very much the aris-tocrat. But Ludendorff was more difficult to assess. Years later the historians would often say that Ludendorff was "a man without a shadow," a phrase from old legends that meant a man without a soul, and thus a man impossible to fathom.

Hindenburg had been briefed by his assistants. They had told him that this Ludendorff was a country gentleman with no connections to the court. He had been raised in a manor by a family of minor nobility. His father had been a cavalry officer in Germany's previous two wars, which were fought against Austria in 1866 and France in 1870. As a youth he had been raised in a home filled with the glories of German arms, statues of German military heroes, and considerable talk about the great Battle of Sedan, where Germany beat France in a famed Battle of Annihilation. This term, beloved by Germany, refers to that rarest of events—the winning of an entire war, or empire, by one single battle. For example, Hannibal tried to do this to Rome at Cannae. And Rome did this to Hannibal at Zama.

When Ludendorff was a boy, his mother's sister tutored him, and then his family sent him off to a cadet school in the town of Plon. He worked ferociously, jumped two grades, and still came in first in his class. He had no friends and no hobbies, but he was a human dynamo in the few fields of study he elected to pursue, and he selected them well. He became an expert in artillery and also in Germany's plan for victory in what they called "the next war." This great plan was the work of Count Alfred von Schlieffen, which had infinite details because it was being constantly revised. These details Ludendorff mastered better than nearly anyone else.

The problem was that this master plan kept changing. For a perfect plan it had strange weaknesses, and vast efforts were made to tweak it. How strong should the left wing invading France be, and how strong the right invading Russia? And what to do if the plan failed? Indeed, was there any provision for failure?

He studied this with infinite detail. Every day he tried to make it perfect. Every part of his day was done by schedule. He was punctual to the minute. He worked constantly and banged his fist on a table when displeased. Reputedly he had no close companions. As one writer remarked, "He had more admirers than friends."

By 1893 he was already at the War Academy, and from there he went on to the General Staff. A glutton for work, he cut through masses of papers to understand what was happening in the war plans of Germany's enemies. There were so many different styles of war that were considered by the Great Powers. The English believed in having a small army and then building it up during a war, for this saved money. The Russians believed in having a staggeringly large army, a veritable "steamroller" of a force, and sending it forth instantly. The French believed in having an army of élan, incredibly mobile and without heavy artillery. The Germans believed in having stupendous artillery to use in the first days of the war. Ludendorff had horrific problems trying to imagine what would happen when these different armies collided. There were so many variables.

Also he had trouble expressing his estimates, for he was not respected. The elites of Germany, pure aristocrats, saw Ludendorff as a problem because he was viewed as a commoner—even though he had a few nobles in his family tree—and worse, he was married to a commoner. His father-in-law actually owned a factory!

In return, Ludendorff disliked the elites. In particular he disliked the Kaiser because he felt the man was a dilettante and worse, because the Kaiser was weak. Kaiser Wilhelm had a deformed body: a mangled hand from birth. Most officers like Ludendorff saw the Kaiser as a cripple.

To his credit, Ludendorff in his studies made herculean efforts to make sense of this "fog of war," and for this he was admired. He was hardworking, ferocious, and dedicated. Some called him a Napoleon because he had taken charge in Belgium and had won victories. And clearly he knew his artillery and the way it could be used to reduce a fortress. His victories in taking the Belgian forts, however delayed, sparked the nation's interest in Ludendorff. He was becoming a popular military leader in what was to become a world war.

This quiet meeting on a railway platform was to have far-reaching results. There was a certain balance between the reserved Hindenburg and the passionate, hardworking young upstart, Ludendorff. As noted by Lieutenant Colonel William A. Jones of the US Army War College in 1992, "It was clear from their first meeting what their respective roles would be. Hindenburg would be the Prussian figurehead for the command and provide the stability necessary for success. . . . This marriage of personalities would endure the entire war." The synergy Hindenburg and Ludendorff created is best expressed by Ludendorff himself when he wrote years later: "For four years the Field Marshal and I worked together like one man in perfect harmony." And with equal affection Hindenburg described his new chief of staff as a man with a "superhuman capacity for work and untiring resolution."

The question that remained for Germany, however, was whether Hindenburg and Ludendorff could deliver a victory against the Russians that would knock them out of the war here and now.

CHAPTER 2

Ludendorff Makes War Against the Russians

NEWS CAME TO the Germans from Russia that their famous invasion plan was having new trouble. The Russians, clearly understanding that France was getting butchered in the West and sensing their panic, decided to sacrifice all caution and to go forward prematurely. Though many Russian soldiers did not have rifles and much of their artillery did not have enough shells, the Russian government sent 600,000 men over the border into East Prussia under the leadership of Generals Alexander Samsonov and Paul von Rennenkampf. These troops were badly armed, mostly untrained, and quite disorganized, but they outnumbered the German soldiers ten to one. Earning the moniker "the Russian steamroller," Samsonov and Rennenkampf's troops swept through East Prussia with reckless courage.

East Prussia was home to the families of many members of the General Staff and was also the ancestral home of the Kaiser, so there was now severe pressure on the royal family to protect these estates. Further, stories of Russian soldiers raping and pillaging swept through Berlin. The tales were almost all fiction—in fact, almost no German women were raped in the invasion—but they alarmed the German High Command. Years later, historians would find evidence in German military archives that the German Army had admitted that "the descriptions of Russian cruelties and the reported devastation of the country are untrue. The Russian troops have everywhere behaved correctly toward the inhabitants. If certain towns and villages have been burned, this was almost always by artillery fire during battle."

The Russians misbehaved only slightly: They liberated every wine cellar they found, and they filled town squares with celebrations. Most annoying to the Germans, they stole incredible quantities of food and large numbers of horses and cows. And most upsetting to German ladies, they would relieve themselves just about anywhere.

So to the west, starting the very first month, the Belgians were resisting far more than the Germans had anticipated; and to the east, the Russians were moving to battle weeks faster than the Germans had believed possible. Clearly they had underestimated their enemies—or they had overestimated their own troops. But at this juncture, luck intervened for the Germans. Only a week after his success at the Battle of Liege, Ludendorff was called by the Kaiser to be chief of staff of the German Eighth Army on the eastern front.

Ludendorff is a terror for biographers. The famous historian Barbara Tuchman, whose 1962 work on the origins of this war, *The Guns of August,* was so good that President Kennedy gave a copy to every member of Congress, researched Ludendorff and found him frustrating. She wished to learn how his mind worked, to find the elements of his persona, but she uncovered almost nothing—there was none of the usual anecdotes. The man was a blank.

But historians have learned more about Ludendorff since the time of Tuchman's book. To start, it is now known that he was clean, obsessively so. Even as a child he would never play a game if it soiled his clothes. Things had to be just so. He liked his academic subjects but not the teachers who taught them. Some people said he was happiest when he was doing mathematics, a science that was unencumbered by people.

He did, however, have the capacity to be sensitive and sentimental, on occasion. Once, as a young man, he shared his umbrella in a Berlin rainstorm with a lovely woman named Margarethe Pernet. Eventually he learned that she was the mother of three boys but was unhappily married, and he developed a bond with her. She liked his passions, and she let him walk her home. Finally he managed to coax her into getting a divorce and marrying him. They shared a dream that they would grow old, their boys becoming officers, their family sitting around the dinner table in peacetime.

Ludendorff then built up his career. He did not take time to exercise, he grew fat, and consequently he had a double chin. At the back of his head there was a bulge, a chunk of fat, which the American writer Ralph Waldo Emerson called "the mark of the beast." He wore a monocle and stared through it in a way that gave people chills. His aides swore that he wore the monocle in his bath.

He never rested. If he stayed up late, he would nonetheless rise early the next day. He would get dressed and be on horseback at 7:00 AM, rain or shine. "Everything was measured in minutes," people said, "not hours."

He became impatient whenever he had to wait. He would come home for luncheon, and if the soup were not on the table, steaming, he would snap, "It is too bad we have no food." He was rude to anyone, even to the Kaiser.

Indeed, he had only one or two friends. And like his future friend Hitler, he blamed everyone else for his failures. People were not just wrong, they were criminally wrong. People were not just stupid, they were treacherously stupid. Things were black and white. He said, "I can only love or hate." Some noted he was better at hating.

He was focused, but he lacked humanity. He hated Jews, then Catholics, finally Christians as a whole. He came to despise Christianity because he said that it made men kind. He preferred the warring gods of old Germany, like Woden, Thor, and Frigg, after whom the days Wednesday, Thursday, and Friday were named. He also despised Judaism because he sensed that the Jews were independent and therefore unpatriotic to Germany.

General Ludendorff did have strengths. His intensity was remarkable. He had a love of Germany. He wanted Germany to be supreme, and to achieve this he urged an outnumbered Germany to wage preventive wars against all potential contenders. At different times he wanted war with England, France, Italy, Poland, Russia, Turkey, and even his ally, Austria-Hungary. He even wanted to go to war with the Vatican. He never put the United States on his list of contenders because he saw Americans as mongrels. He believed them to be so inexperienced that they would never be a threat. This was perhaps the greatest mistake of his life.

He never once tried to reduce the numbers of his enemies in Germany. He never saw that his enemies might be coaxed into being friends. Indeed historians have been hard-pressed to find any friends at all.

He hated authority. One would assume that he respected the Kaiser, his commander in chief, but he did not. He respected the fatherland in a vague sense, but that was all. Over time he would become the only one in the German Empire to bully the Kaiser. Ultimately he was similar to the French king who was alleged to have said, "I am the state."

For a time his approach worked. Ludendorff went from being a nobody to being the commander of half the German armies in the new world war. He instantly became the hero of the hour. When he was sent to Russia, he knew that if he scored a second victory, it would make his reputation, even among the elites who scorned him for being a commoner.

The train sped Ludendorff east. In his pocket he carried the letter from the chief of the German General Staff appointing him to head the Eighth Army and urging him to avert the crisis in Russia. Everyone believed that the situation was desperate and that the Russians might win. Ludendorff scoured his reports, but they gave no clear indication of what was happening or what kind of hand he held. Despite this lack of information, Ludendorff would have agreed with a rising colonel named Douglas MacArthur back in America who would ever assert, "It's not the cards you are dealt, but how you play them."

Eventually Ludendorff learned that the Eighth Army was outnumbered and in retreat, and that 600,000 Russians were on German soil, coming near. The number of advancing troops was chilling. But Ludendorff wondered, were these 600,000 men ace troops or militia? Veterans or conscripts? An army or a mob?

These questions were serious, given the recent history of the Russian military. In 1905, the huge Russian Army had been unprepared and had performed poorly against Japan. At the confused Battle of Mukden in Manchuria, whole Russian armies had

stumbled against one another, going to the wrong places and fir-
ing on one another. Their leaders had given contradictory orders,
everyone swirling in the smoke and achieving little. Some generals blamed their fellow officers for failing to support each other
in what was, clearly, the most important land battle of that war.
Meanwhile some 10,000 Russian sailors were casualties on the
high seas in the Strait of Tsushima. Clearly, Russian forces had performed badly in 1905. Worse, they had sparked a near-revolution
in Russia. Back home, an entire Russian city, Odessa, had gone
over to the revolutionaries.

Now, in 1914, the Germans wondered how skilled these
600,000 soldiers were. If these Russian troops were moving fast
and were unprepared, they would offer Germany an opportunity.
One deliberate German division, managed by men of cool nerves,
might do miracles.

The two German generals, Ludendorff and Hindenburg, now
talked soldier to soldier, and they must have been struck by how
much they had in common. They were both disciples of the great
Schlieffen, whose plan ruled the day. They both dreamed of a Battle
of Annihilation that would win the war in hours. They both were
traditional German military men who believed in the mystical power of the German race.

The egotistical Kaiser disliked Hindenburg. During the annual
maneuvers in 1908, when the Germans were still trying to perfect
the problematic Schlieffen Plan, Hindenburg had refused to let the
Kaiser win a particular encounter. Hindenburg, with dangerous
candor, had quipped, "If this were war, you would be my prisoner." Kaiser Wilhelm II had been humiliated. From that moment,
he shunned Hindenburg at court.

So the two generals were outsiders going off to seek their fortunes. Their commonalities made for a good beginning, and their qualities complemented one another. Hindenburg was calmness and intellect, while Ludendorff was fire and action. Hindenburg was a creature of character, quiet and deep, while Ludendorff was a man of passion, aggressive and engaged. People would soon refer to their relationship as "a union," even "a marriage." Soon the press would call them The Duo. Whether their marriage would last was a question for the future. Whether they would save Germany was the question of the hour.

On their train ride east, they were amazed by the high spirits of the troops around them, all with flowers on their rifles, singing old German tunes like "The Watch on the Rhine," taken from a poem of 1840:

> Oh fatherland, no fear be thine,
> Firm stands the watch, upon the Rhine.

And then "Deutschland über alles," with a hint of a threat:

> Germany, Germany above everything
> Above everything in the world . . .

When the train got the generals to Prussia, they were met by their new staff, and here they had luck. Amid these officers, one colonel, Max Hoffmann, seemed to know every detail concerning the advancing Russians. Hoffmann was an experienced officer who had previously served as the German military observer assigned to the Japanese forces in that nation's war with Russia in 1905. His experience in that conflict would prove invaluable in understanding the Russians' movements in Prussia.

Hoffmann provided new information about the advancing Russian enemy. First, there was not one Russian Army of 600,000 men. Rather, there were two separate armies of 300,000 each. They were divided and were not in close communication with one another. For German generals who believed in the sainted von Schlieffen, this was a gift. They were fighting a divided command, just like Hannibal in ancient times before his greatest victory.

The Russian mobilization was reckless. They were unprepared and disorganized, and they did not have enough rifles, ammunition, horses, or food. The czar had decided to rescue his French allies at any price, and he was sending this suicide mission into Germany to frighten the Prussians and upset their timetable.

One of the two Russian armies was commanded by General Alexander Samsonov, a hardworking public servant who had been in the czar's army for over thirty years. He was a tough cavalry officer who had fought the Turks, Chinese, Japanese, and now the Germans. There were those who heard him boast that he had not read a military manual in years, and some asserted that he did not have an analytical bone in his body. But everyone agreed that he was brave. He was a veteran of the disastrous Battle of Mukden in Manchuria in 1905, which would turn out to be desperately important.

The second Russian army was commanded by a more intellectual fellow named Paul von Rennenkampf, a veteran of forty years and a man of intellect. Long before he had been graduated first in his class at his military academy. He too was a veteran of that disaster in Manchuria almost ten years before. And what was intriguing to Hoffmann was that the two Russian generals hated each other. Samsonov felt that Rennenkampf had abandoned him at the critical moment in 1905 and had butchered his troops by his intentional absence.

Later the two met on a railway platform in Manchuria, and they got into a fight like schoolboys. Slugging, cursing, screaming, spitting, and biting, they fell over one another in the mud, tearing at each other's hair, medals, eyeglasses, and buttons.

Several observers shared the story about their tussle, and many people heard about it, including Max Hoffmann. Hoffmann suspected that the two generals would sabotage each other if given the chance. And Hoffmann said that this hostility provided his fellow Germans with a golden opportunity. In all probability the one Russian general would not rescue the other, so the Germans would be able to fight them one at a time, and destroy them piecemeal.

The Russian mobilization was premature. Vast numbers of inexperienced peasants had been conscripted, declared to be an army, and sent forward. Most had no weapons because more than 100,000 rifles had been rushed to Serbia, a nation that was hit earlier in the war. An experienced Russian officer at the time could not conceal his disgust.

"What a way to go to war," he sighed. "Just look at these half-starved peasants. Most have never fired a shot. We crawl along on bare feet and get our troops tired before the battle starts. Marshes to our left and right, nothing but water and broken forests. What good is it to have four times as many men as the enemy? We cannot deploy them. Take one step off this road and you drown. Our army will attack bunched up, and on a narrow front. The Germans know this and wait with heavy artillery. They have discovered what modern war is all about. I fear we may have to pay a heavy price."

The Russians were good young men, but their orders were con-
flicting. The army had trouble putting orders into code. Their so-
lution was unfortunate. They began sending orders in the clear,
without encoding them. This meant that the Germans could eaves-
drop on everything the Russians were saying. Later Hoffmann told
it plain: "We had an ally, the enemy. We knew all the enemy's
plans."

Given Hoffmann's familiarity with the Russians and with perfect intelligence regarding the Russians' current orders, Hindenburg
and Ludendorff could now attack the enemy armies one at a time.
The Germans, though outnumbered, would have an advantage.
In each battle the faster-moving Germans, at the point of contact,
would have more troops than the Russians. In this sense they would
outnumber the Russians. They would wipe out the first half of the
enemy forces, then the second.

But before Ludendorff and Hindenburg could set this plan into
action, events in France intervened. The German armies there were
finally doing well, advancing swiftly, and decimating the French.
In the first encounter, known as the Battle of the Frontiers, the
Germans inflicted 260,000 casualties in just the first month.

This success in France was striking, and many German officers
were saying that the French were finished. And now, because there
was worry in Berlin about the Russian advance into East Prussia,
the chief of staff of the German Army, von Moltke, made a fateful
decision. In what some consider the great German error of the war,
von Moltke moved three infantry corps and one cavalry division
from the French front in the West to the Russian front in the East.

When von Moltke's staff telephoned these tidings to Ludendorff,
the general was surprised. Ludendorff did not feel that he needed

the troops, and, more relevantly, he was nearly certain that they would not arrive in time to take part in the fighting. Of course he would accept them—generals do not turn down reinforcements. The high command scaled back the number of soldiers a little, leaving out one of the three infantry corps, but sent the rest.

By accepting these elite troops Ludendorff weakened the effectiveness of the Schlieffen Plan in France. And by allowing the troops to be sent on that day, Ludendorff ensured that they would not arrive in time to do battle. Ludendorff probably felt he did nothing wrong in accepting these troops. But these soldiers, now neutralized, could have continued the fight in France where they were going to be needed.

So it was that on August 28, 1914, Ludendorff and Hindenburg began their most famous campaign. Hoffmann had a perfect battle plan drawn up, and all Hindenburg and Ludendorff had to do was carry it out. But Ludendorff ordered Hoffmann to attack before the men and artillery were in place. Hoffmann with aplomb ignored Ludendorff for hours. Carefully he lured the Russians forward, and only when he had poor Samsonov surrounded did he unleash the fury of his mechanized German Army.

The Russian soldiers, who were starving and barefoot, did try to fight. Those without rifles rushed about the field looking for dead soldiers whose weapons they could use. Others, low on ammo, opened dead soldiers' kit bags for bullets.

The Russian artillery ran out of ammunition first, the Cossacks ran out second, and the rank and file third. By evening, Samsonov's army was annihilated. The poor fellows did not know where they were or where to go. Most of the men in Samsonov's force were dying or captured, and only 8,000 managed to smash through the python-like encirclement. Once they broke free, they wandered the forests, looking at the stars, trying to calculate where to go.

It looked like a disastrous Russian defeat. But in truth, Samsonov only appeared defeated. He had still managed to serve his nation: He had been sent on a suicide mission to frighten the Prussians in the East and to destabilize the Schlieffen Plan, and this he had done. What the Belgians had started, by upsetting the Schlieffen timetable, Samsonov and his ill-prepared troops had finished. By invading Prussia, the Russians had gotten the German High Command to detach 80,000 troops from the spearhead of their forces in France. Now the timetable would really collapse, and the German plan to defeat France in four weeks and then Russia in four months was ruined. This in turn meant that Germany was now fighting a two-front war, the kind that Germany could not win.

The Germans understood nothing of this. Instead, Germany was electrified by the news of the decisive battle in the East, the thousands of enemy soldiers dead, the broken wagons, the captured artillery, the battle flags, the gory glory of it all. The German Army called it the Battle of Tannenberg to commemorate a moment there in 1410 when German knights had been badly defeated by a Polish and Lithuanian force. This victory in 1914 they saw as vengeance.

Fantastic tales grew, and even some military jokes were told. Hoffmann, talking about how the battle was lost because of an old grudge between the two officers fighting on the railway platform, put it this way: "If it is true that the Battle of Waterloo was won on the playing fields of Eton, so it is also true that the Battle of Tannenberg was lost on that wretched railway platform in Manchuria."

Though Samsonov bought France and Russia time and had thus upset the Schlieffen Plan, he did not realize it, and the man was miserable. He had lost many thousands of men, and thousands more were surrendering. This fine general of old Russia, with his years of service, did not know how he could face the czar after such a debacle. He walked away in silence, and then his men heard a shot.

They could not find his body in the dark.

Soon the German Command began to manufacture sparkling legends about the victory at Tannenberg. Myths began to spring up. Stories evolved about thousands of Russian soldiers forced into a swamp, up to their chins in muck, drowning in the filth and begging for mercy. They were alleged to have shouted, "Comrade! Comrade!" as they sank. The stories were false—no Russian armies drowned in the swamps—but the tale expanded, and eventually the returning soldiers were coaxed into saying how they could hear the screams of the Russians every day and would hear them forever.

The German High Command began to inflate the number of the Russian dead at Tannenberg and to reduce the number of the German dead to convince average Germans that they had had an even greater victory. Eventually, the Germans raised millions for Berlin architects Johannes and Walter Krüger to design and build a monument to this victory near the site of the battle. It was a huge brooding work inspired by Stonehenge in England, consisting of massive prehistoric towers seventy-five feet high and a circular wall enclosing a solemn space big enough for thousands of people to worship in nearly religious fashion.

The Tannenberg memorial was dedicated in 1924 and finished in 1927. It was meant to last thousands of years to show the greatness of the German Army. But alas, it was destroyed in World

War II. Hitler's troops, seeing the approaching Russian forces in 1945, blasted it apart. Later, peasants looted the rubble, seeking the bronze and granite to use for building materials. Then the Polish government razed the little that was left to build their Palace of Culture and Science in Warsaw. Today nothing remains of this eternal monument but grassy knolls, and no visitor would guess that this was something once considered glorious.

Eventually scholars followed the High Command's lead and convinced themselves that this battle was a gigantic success for Germany. A reference book by renowned scholars Spencer C. Tucker and Priscille Mary Roberts smoothly says: "Tannenberg was perhaps Germany's greatest military success of the War and conversely one of the greatest of Russia's military defeats." Every German took pride in the victory and imagined, *If we can beat the Russians like this, we can win the war.*

Their confidence was high, but it was so high that three devastating points were ignored: First, the Schlieffen Plan had failed. The prime element was a great German surge that would sweep all around Paris and would capture both the city of Paris and the bulk of the French Army, all at once, an awesome feat that would be impossible to achieve with the number of soldiers available, especially when 80,000 men had been subtracted from the equation. Second, the plan's rigorous timetable was impossible, for it demanded superhuman precision, and that was why it broke down during the first days of the war, in both the East and the West. Third, the apparent Allied defeats had stopped the German war of movement, which was Germany's only hope. The conflict was soon collapsing into trench warfare, which would favor the defender so thoroughly that no breakthrough could take place. Tanks, which could have broken through, had not yet been invented. Therefore the result would be a grinding and brutal stalemate, with staggering losses.

Few in Germany understood this. An exception was Walter Rathenau, the most brilliant German industrialist at the time, who felt that this so-called victory of Tannenberg was based on false assumptions and erroneous interpretations. He also sensed that Germany was doomed. Highly educated in physics, chemistry, and philosophy, the brilliant Rathenau began to work for the Raw Materials Department of the War Ministry and did his all to put the German economy on a solid footing. But he worried that a single country like Germany could never win a drawn-out war against the machines of Britain, Russia, and France.

Years later, Dr. Roger Chickering, an ace professor of German history at Georgetown University, came to the same conclusion. Chickering noted in an interview with the authors of this book that "Germany's military success in 1914 was a failure. They did not knock out France in four weeks and did not knock out Russia in four months. Therefore they got bogged down in a two-front war, a war of attrition, the kind that Germany was bound to lose."

Fortunately for Ludendorff, most Germans could not see how bad things were. And so the first phase of the war ended with Germany enshrining Ludendorff and Hindenburg as their two national heroes, confident that the future belonged to them and that the war would be over soon, when in fact it would last for years and become the most ferocious struggle the world had ever known.

CHAPTER 3

Ludendorff's Road to Power

G ERMANY WAS IN chaos. Everywhere there was slaughter in the trenches, and everywhere Ludendorff announced victories to a grateful nation. He handled his figures adroitly, inflating the number of enemy dead while never releasing the total number of German dead. He made known the *local* number of German dead, the boys in this or that town who had died; it was the *national* total that he concealed. He could not permit anyone to sense that in this war of numbers, against so many empires, Germany was destined to lose.

Ludendorff and Hindenburg excelled at this kind of numbers cooking. In the Battle of the Masurian Lakes against Russia, on September 20, 1914, for example, The Duo killed 56,000 enemy soldiers but claimed they took 110,000 lives. It is unclear whether this dissembling was conscious on their part or if their staff kept them in the dark and fed cooked numbers to them. Both the Kaiser and Ludendorff were insulated from the truth, and Ludendorff in turn kept the Kaiser doubly isolated. Strangely, none of these powerful men, however intelligent, realized that Germany had really lost the world war in the first four months. That realization would require four years.

Another problem was the overconfidence of Ludendorff and his circle. These Germans believed that they were racially superior to their enemies—they believed they were a masterful race. This dreadful idea of racial superiority, the idea of a "master race," a term that seems to have been invented in 1836 in Virginia, where whites saw themselves as the natural masters and saw blacks as the God-ordained slaves, was adopted by the Germans to such a degree that it overwhelmed their military ideas. They thought the Russians were inferior stock, while the French were arty but decadent, and the English were impressive, yes, but foolish when compared to civilized Germans. And the Americans were mongrels, beneath contempt. The Germans believed, amid all these illusions, that they were the only triumphant race on the planet. Indeed it would take two world wars and tens of millions of dead to disabuse them of these illusions.

But every time the Germans gained a victory in World War I, triumph eluded them. Meanwhile their cultured youth, some of the best in Europe, were drafted into the army and driven to swift despair. One young man, the violinist Fritz Kreisler, described how he became a killing machine in this brave new world of Ludendorff's war.

"Centuries drop away from you. You become a primeval sort of man. For twenty-one days I went without taking off my clothes, sleeping in the mud or in the swamps. Many things you once saw as requirements of civilization just dropped out of existence. A toothbrush became unimaginable. We learned to eat by instinct . . . with our hands. Soon we all looked like lean shaggy wolves, from the necessity of subsisting on next to nothing. I remember having gone more than three days without food, and many a time we had to lick the dew from the grass because we had no water. You felt a fierceness arising in you, an indifference to anything the world holds, except your duty of fighting. . . . Why am I here trying to kill someone I've never seen before in my life?"

Kreisler became so disgusted with Ludendorff's war that he escaped to New York and stayed there until his death in 1962. He forgot his life as a wolf and became a beloved artist. He was one of the lucky ones.

Back in the trenches the men tried hard to maintain their humanity, especially that first year. That first Christmas of 1914, the soldiers on the western front did a startling thing. Contrary to the rules, they effected a temporary truce, one that the generals did not approve. It started when the British sentries saw the Germans putting tiny Christmas trees along the top of their trenches. Said British sergeant A. Lovell of the Third Rifle Brigade: "They've got Christmas trees all along the top of their trenches! Never saw such a sight!"

One German put out a banner that read, *Happy Christmas!*

Then one Englishman shouted, "Hello, Fritz! Come halfway!"

Spontaneously the troops got together under a white flag, and they exchanged cigarettes and coffee, beer here, whisky there, chocolate here, candy there. Amid a wilderness of shattered trees and sinkholes, they sang different versions of "Silent Night," the one song they all knew, which brought them together. Then they showed one another the pictures of the girls they left behind. In several instances, Belgian soldiers came forward with letters to loved ones in their German-occupied homeland and asked enemy soldiers to please see if these could be delivered. Almost always the Germans did just that. And both sides played soccer against one another, as best they could—for the landscape was so gutted by bombs that the men had to work to find a level field.

Many Englishmen wanted permission, during this one Christmas truce, to go over the battlefield and seek out the cadavers of friends who had fallen recently, which no one had been able to retrieve. The Germans were incredibly kind, not only giving permission but actually going out and helping the English to dig countless graves in the mud and then to lower the rotting bodies into the pits. It only happened this one Christmas, but this kindness was remarkable.

Most soldiers were enchanted by the decency of their enemy. One exception was a lance corporal from Austria named Adolf Hitler, who said, "One should not fraternize with the enemy in any war." As Sir Ian Kershaw of England has noted in his superb 904-page biography of the man, Hitler was ferocious in hating Germany's enemies, even during a truce, and was horrified by this fraternization. There was also an aloof young French officer named Charles de Gaulle who found the spectacle of fraternization to be "regrettable." But these two zealous soldiers were the exception.

Ludendorff raged over this truce, this act of indiscipline, and he made plans to see that it never happened again. But whatever he felt, there was one question that the soldiers did ask one another: "Why are we doing this to each other?"

No one knew how to end this war. This stalemate went on because no one could stop it. Some British generals talked of placing mines under the trenches of the enemy and blowing them sky high. On one occasion at a village in Belgian West Flanders called Messines, the Allies ignited 455 tons of explosives some seventy-five feet underground, making a roar heard across the Channel.

But it did not stop the war because nothing stopped the war. The war expanded, and it was harder and harder for any country to maintain neutrality. Groups that had no business fighting for either side, such as Romania, Portugal, and the Ottoman Empire, were pressured to join one killing machine or another.

The war continued unabated, and the pressures only worsened. The British Navy covered the German coast and stopped the import of all food and supplies in what became the greatest blockade in history. This caused enormous problems. For a time the German government, by the strictest rationing, fed everyone. Still, wise men warned Ludendorff that the British were tightening the blockade every month, and with the government drafting so many farmers to fight in the war, the nation's food supply was breaking down, and Germany could starve.

But Ludendorff, sensing victory around every corner, would not heed. He was like a compulsive gambler who, whatever his losses, convinces himself that he can win everything back with one last throw of the dice. In this way, trench war continued inexorably, as if it were a Moloch, and the numbers of dead increased daily. More and more men who were sacrificed were civilians, especially the young and old. And people were starving. The Carnegie Endowment for International Peace would finally estimate that 600,000 Germans died as a result of malnutrition during the war, but this was merely a guess. The only certainty was that starvation was taking place. Civilians had a hard time finding food, and a black market began to flourish.

The rats were having an easy time finding food, however, for there was always an extra body in No Man's Land. The lice were having a splendid time too and were reproducing in the trillions. Life in the trenches was so bad that some men sought out whores near the front because they wanted a diseased person to infect them, so the doctors would send them to the hospitals for a time.

The wolves too were having an unusual season, coming down from the hills in the dark to eat men in No Man's Land—a paralyzed young man in No Man's Land was their ideal delicacy. And his screams did not bother the wolves or rats even a little.

But this new war was worst for the horses of England. More than 2,000 died every *week*, screaming, their middles often torn open, entrails dangling as they ran across the muddy fields in agony. Many were hit by machine gun fire, many were tangled in the barbed wire, and more were torn by the invention of an English soldier named Henry Shrapnel, for the bits of shrapnel ravaged them massively. All in all some 500,000 horses were doomed to die in this war, but that is only an estimate. The true number may have been greater.

Amid the fighting, the men could sometimes relax for a few hours. A German soldier could go off to a whorehouse run by the army for a frantic coupling, and he did not have to pay any money. But the girl he selected would be a poor refugee from some place like Romania, with whom he could not even communicate, and she would be distant. It was all absentminded and quick. What more was there to say? Such was the world of Ludendorff's army in the midst of the greatest slaughter in history, and it went on because no one could stop it. Indeed, no one even tried.

For two years Ludendorff and Hindenburg claimed to win their victories on the Russian front. But there was such confusion, such war without end, and such uncertainty. To make it more logical and sane, the generals tried to lobby the Kaiser into making one ironclad decision. They wanted to know if victory would be sought primarily in the East or the West, because they wanted to know where they should put the greater effort. The officers pressed the Kaiser to answer for two long years.

From 1914 to 1916 there was a growing feeling among most German elites that victory would first come on the western front. The elites who held this belief were called the Westerners, and they were adamant that the Russians could wait. The Germans should defeat the British and French in the West, and only then should they turn to the Russians upon the eastern front and finish them off. The Russians, isolated, would collapse, and Germany would win the war.

Ludendorff took the opposite view. He and the Easterners, those who believed victory would come first on the eastern front, felt that the Russians were the weak link in the Allied chain, and there he wanted to strike, hard and repeatedly, month after month, until they were dead. Also he felt a need to be powerful in the East to bolster the Austrian allies, whom he saw as the weak link in his chain.

So the Westerners and the Easterners bickered. The leader of the Westerners, General Erich von Falkenhayn, caused Ludendorff concern. Falkenhayn, reputed to be one of the most realistic military minds in Germany, told anyone who would listen that Germany could not have it all. Germany would have to limit its ambitions because its soldiers could not win both in the East and the West. Falkenhayn wanted a limited victory in the war and a separate peace with Russia. He did not believe in an earth-shattering triumph. He just wanted to win the war and go home.

This was heresy to both Hindenburg and Ludendorff, who were getting lost in dreams of glory and in the idea of making Germany the greatest power in the world.

But Falkenhayn then made a miscalculation that would kill hundreds of thousands of men. He convinced the Westerners that they could bait the French into a fatal battle at a place called Verdun, and there the Germans would inflict such losses that the French would sue for peace. Falkenhayn was sure that the Germans would inflict more casualties than they would receive, because a railroad supplied the German side of Verdun, with only a narrow roadway serving the French side. With plans for the German railroad delivering vast stores of munitions and men and countless rounds of artillery, the Westerners convinced themselves that they could cripple the French and win the war in this one last battle.

Later generations of historians came to despise this strategy. Oxford-trained World War I historian Jehuda Wallach, who did extraordinary work as a revered military historian at the head of the History Department at Tel Aviv University, scorned Falkenhayn's "satanic attitude of sacrificing hundreds of thousands of their own soldiers to kill or cripple twice that number of the enemy."

For a while Falkenhayn was in the ascendant. The Germans began their ploy at Verdun and at first seemed to succeed. The French took the bait and sent thousands of men into this cauldron. The Germans brought in men and munitions on the railway as planned, and the railway boxcars even had those wonderful ball bearings on the floor, an invention they learned from the American circus guru P. T. Barnum, which made it easy to unload cargo swiftly. The Germans were sure they could slaughter the French with ease.

But the Germans were again far too overconfident. By awesome work, French truck drivers delivered 54,000 tons of munitions and supplies, plus 260,000 men, just the first month. Further, no truck was broken down for more than two minutes, for the French had swarms of mechanics ready to fix anything along the road. The French opened quarries nearby to supply crushed stone to widen the road, and soon there were supply trucks arriving at Verdun every fourteen seconds. To this day the French call the road to Verdun "the Sacred Way," as indeed it was.

A French novelist, Henri Barbusse, called the battle "The Fire," and that name was appropriate too. The Germans, with huge advantages, did fight well, but the French fought more fiercely because the life of their nation was in jeopardy. Even though they were outgunned, even though the poison gas of France was not as crippling as the German gas, and even though they were drowning in their own blood, the French kept coming. They shouted the battle cry from Joan of Arc, "On les aura!" and kept moving forward, fighting in the shell craters, fighting under the light of the moon, fighting amid the wolves and the rats. There were no intellectual calculations or radical formulae, there was just the ferocious struggle of a wounded nation. And when it was over, the Germans were aghast to find that they had lost about as many as the French.

For all their clever plans, the Germans had a draw. There were 278,000 German casualties and 460,000 French casualties. So it was that the German victory at Verdun was hollow. It was "a vanity bloodbath," the cynics quipped. The dream of the Westerners became a nightmare for all. A battle resulting in more than 700,000 casualties went beyond the imagination of a civilized person. War was not supposed to be like this. The Americans had won the Revolutionary War with a mere 7,000 battlefield deaths. That was the *old* way of war; it was elegant and refined. They did not even fight in the winter, for that simply was not done. They did not have to jail a captive. The captive would give his word, his "parole," that he would not fight again, and he would then be allowed to go home. And when they did fight, and won an engagement, they would invite the enemy officers to dinner, in a courteous wish to salute them for a battle well fought. This was the old way of war, as genteel as a game of chess.

The new way of war was brutally different. It had death numbers that tolled chillingly, like the church bells of an old cathedral, and it involved numbing losses that went on forever. To paraphrase an epigram from a Roman philosopher, these men were making a desert and calling it peace.

At Verdun, there were more than 700,000 casualties, on both sides, for zero results. And this was not the only battle of this time that had such casualties. Another battle of similar ferocity took place between the Austro-Hungarians and the Russians, with combined casualties of 339,000. It happened in 1915, in the Carpathian Mountains on the Polish–Hungarian border, where the Austro-Hungarian general Franz Conrad von Hötzendorf sent his troops against the Russians in a grandiose battle. It is a tale as heartbreaking as the Battle of Verdun.

Amid snowdrifts that were eight feet high, in cold so severe that a soldier had to thaw his rifle before he used it, in blizzards so intense that a man who fell asleep might never awaken, the Austro-Hungarians sent their long-suffering troops to fight Russia. From ledges in the mountains, the Russians would roll barrels of dynamite upon the Austro-Hungarians, scattering them like bowling pins. In the forests, the Austro-Hungarians would hear the howling of wolves, which, some claimed, ate soldiers alive.

The Austro-Hungarians were starving, for they were not able to bring in much food by horse and mule. And they were freezing, for the temperature was twenty degrees below zero at night. Yet they held their one great fortress, Przemysl, for much of the year. Fifteen thousand Russian bodies lay around this fortress, scattered like broken dolls, proof of the tenacity of this army.

But the Austro-Hungarian fortress eventually collapsed. On March 23, 1915, just before surrendering, the soldiers destroyed their vehicles, phones, telegraphs, and artillery and killed the last of their horses. Only then did they give up. Nine generals and 117,000 enlisted men surrendered. The emperor of Austria-Hungary wept when the fortress fell.

In total the battles of 1915 and 1916 saw hundreds of thousands of useless casualties as a result of Germany's acts, and in all this upheaval, Ludendorff craftily saw an opportunity. The Westerners were discredited, and Ludendorff was ready to make a play for greater power, to achieve total command of the German armies. The able aide Colonel Max Hoffmann wrote how at this time Hindenburg was rarely asking about military operations and how Ludendorff was now assuming command: "Ludendorff directs everything, Hindenburg learning about it for the most part much later." The aide went further: "Here we generally sign the orders 'Hindenburg' without having shown them to him at all. . . . Ludendorff does everything himself."

Ludendorff's power play was working. After the failure of Verdun, during the last days of 1916, Ludendorff wrote a letter to the Kaiser, a letter that Hindenburg delivered, arguing that Falkenhayn no longer enjoyed the confidence of the army and that Hindenburg did. The losses everywhere, the letter claimed, were the worst in history. Something had to be done, and the generals wanted action.

The Kaiser was bewildered during these blood-drenched days. He could not sleep, and he spent his time reading novels. He said that he had been betrayed by England and could not understand why his fellow monarchs should plot his destruction. When he was especially gloomy, he went to the battlefield of Sedan, where

Germany won its great victory against France in 1870. And there he brooded. He was obsessed with his country's victory there, when the Germans had maneuvered the French as if on a chessboard, until they had them where they wanted them. The Germans had dominated the French so perfectly that one French officer offered the celebrated description, "We are in the center of a toilet, and they are going to shit on us!"

The Kaiser wanted a victory like this, but there was none. Germany was failing, and its glories were failing too. Germany and its allies were enduring the worst battles of history. Even when Germany seemed to win a battle, there were terrible losses that they could not replace. Truth to tell, for Germany, *attrition* was just another word for *defeat*.

The Kaiser had to do something better or he would go down in history as a clown. And he knew that if Germany lost, he would lose his throne. Vast numbers of British talked of trying the Kaiser in court when they won the war. And no matter how severe this war, the British were convinced that they were going to win it.

The Kaiser was collapsing, a shadow of the man he should have been. The poor fellow was only the caretaker of his estates, wandering through his thirty-one empty palaces like Lear on his heath, raging about the injustice of it all and wondering where it would end.

So it was in January of 1917 that the Kaiser was forced to demote Falkenhayn and to promote Ludendorff and Hindenburg beyond what they merited. He made Hindenburg the chief of the general staff and Ludendorff first quartermaster general. This was hard for him because the Kaiser now despised Ludendorff, convinced that the man was of "dubious character, and eaten away by ambition." Yet the Kaiser felt he could not do without these two, for the army's propaganda agencies had convinced the nation that these two generals were the key to success. In many ways Germany was trapped by its own words.

So Ludendorff now became the top military man in Germany, in control of Hindenburg and in charge of the war. To some it seemed that the Kaiser was ruining his throne to preserve his throne.

In the madhouse of this war, many Germans saw the promotions as necessary. The public was happy, for at this brief moment, Hindenburg and Ludendorff had reached their peak of popularity. The army was glad, for they saw victory on the horizon. The Social Democrats were happy, for they saw a victory that should cost less than Verdun. And the skeptics were pleased, because they saw Ludendorff as a good choice because he was immune from court influence.

Only one important individual conspicuously disagreed with promoting Ludendorff: a prescient Colonel von Marschall. The colonel was a mild-mannered member of the Kaiser's cabinet, with years of experience. And he hated Ludendorff. Said his aides: "He feared that Ludendorff in his measureless vanity and pride would conduct the war until the German people were completely exhausted, and [that Ludendorff would then] let the monarchy bear the damages." Indeed, he said that Ludendorff would "destroy Germany."

But his was a voice in the wilderness. No one sounded the alarm. Indeed no one seemed to understand all that was happening. And what was happening was this: Ludendorff had engineered a military coup. From 1916 to the war's end, Ludendorff would dominate Germany. He now had power over the Kaiser and over Hindenburg. And now that he had this power, the chilling question was, What would he do with it?

CHAPTER 4
Ludendorff Attacks in 1916

WORLD WAR I was not the same conflict in 1916 that it had been in 1914. And Germany was not the same nation. Much had changed after two years of total war. In 1916 the people of Germany lived in a reality so different from anything they had known that they could hardly recognize themselves or what their country had become.

Germany was dying—not the Germany of Ludendorff's soldiers, for they received first priority for all food and supplies—but the Germany of the civilians, the public at large. The people were suffering more than Ludendorff and his fellow generals seemed to know. There were such extreme shortages of potatoes that most people had to make do with turnips, and the end of 1916 became known as the Turnip Winter.

Civilians put up a brave front. Ernesta Drinker of Philadelphia, a blueblood married to a future US ambassador, chanced to visit Germany in this time and was surprised to find that if a young soldier died in the war, the neighbors would try to congratulate the family on its sacrifice and would pretend that these were grounds for rejoicing. But by 1916 there were millions dead and no reasons to rejoice, and the congratulations sounded hollow.

By 1916 German boys had stopped growing, mostly due to the starvation inflicted by the British blockade. A report issued later by the Carnegie Endowment for International Peace said that about 150,000 Germans died of starvation every year of the war. It could not be otherwise, for the food that was produced in Germany was mostly sent to the military. Ludendorff's drafting of farmers into the army was another reason supplies dwindled. But the most insidious reason was Ludendorff's confiscating the chemicals previously utilized to make fertilizer and instead using them to make countless canisters of poison gas.

This gas was created by a doctor named Fritz Haber, a chemist who would in 1919 receive a Nobel Prize, despite the mass murder in which he was engaged. His poison gases were so efficient that they could penetrate enemy masks and kill men wearing what had once been adequate equipment. But even Haber warned Ludendorff that Germany could endure only one more year without fertilizer, and therefore Ludendorff had only months to win the war. After one more year there would be so many civilian casualties, so many starving, that they would have little left to fight for. Ludendorff shrugged, demanded discipline, and did as he pleased.

The new gases were acidic and inflamed the lungs. In one battle Ludendorff and Haber released 168 *tons* of chlorine gas. Haber killed so many young men from England, France, and Russia that his wife, Clara, who had a doctorate in physical chemistry and understood what these chemicals did to a boy's lungs, told Haber that she despised him for maiming the youth of Europe.

She did not know all the details—no one knew—but one of the poor boys who would be mauled by her husband's gases was a young lance corporal of the Sixteenth Bavarian Regiment whose mind now suffered from what they called "hysterical blindness" from the gas attacks in Belgium. The boy was a troubled youth named Adolf Hitler.

Clara Haber also hated her husband for taking a commission in the German Army and for becoming such a zealous captain. She hated to see him in uniform. And the way he wore his revolver at all times nauseated her. He was so proud of his elegant appearance that he pursued affairs with superficial women, the kind of women who were impressed with such things. It was widely known that he was having an affair with his secretary, a vapid woman named Charlotte. This was not the man Clara had married, and Germany was not the nation where she had been raised. If he were decent, Clara insisted, he would refuse to engage in this cannibalism. He was a Jew, she reminded him, and presumably a civilized person like herself.

Haber, a superpatriot, accused her of treason. He felt that everyone, Jew or Christian, should do everything possible for victory. Clara, a clean-cut daughter of a farmer, screamed that patriotism and religion had nothing to do with it. It was a matter of honor, and he should try to be a civilized man.

Fritz then stormed out in his handsome uniform, and Clara, after sobbing over his crimes, took one of his service revolvers, went into their garden, and shot herself in the chest. Her son Hermann, a gentle thirteen-year-old boy, rushed out to find her dying. He held her in his arms while the blood went out of her.

The evil unleashed in this family, beginning with Dr. Haber's poison gases, continued to grow over time. Well after World War I, Haber's brilliant assistants helped make more poison gases, which were used at Auschwitz to kill more people, including some of

Haber's relatives! And Haber's son Hermann, when he understood how many millions of Jews his father's gases had murdered, killed himself for shame. The senior Haber was the only lucky one. He received the Nobel Prize in 1919, and then he later died peacefully in Switzerland. It was an easy life for a monster.

The Germans managed to inflict stupendous casualties on vast numbers of their adversaries the first few times they used Haber's gases, in 1915, but they paid a price, because soon the civilized world saw Germans as barbarians. Eventually Germans were seen as what men of ancient Rome had called "enemies of the human race."

Then the situation worsened for Germany on the battlefield. The Allies began to develop their own poison gases to retaliate, and they found they had a geographical advantage. Because the winds in Europe mostly blow from west to east, the gases of the Allies were more effective against the Germans than the Germans' gases had been on them. Inevitably there were more days when the wind went against them, as the Germans were horrified to discover.

The situation worsened even more on the home front. With the lack of chemicals to produce fertilizer, rations fell. By 1916 the diet of a German adult had dropped to 1,000 calories a day, enough for only a child of three. Soon more Germans were starving, and many, half starved and weakened, died from diseases like dysentery and tuberculosis. Life became frantic. In 1916 alone, some 121,000 Germans were listed as having starved to death, and this was a conservative estimate.

Most German children could not go to school because there was no coal to heat the classrooms. Besides, the young needed to spend their days seeking supplies for their families. They went down to the depots to try to salvage even one piece of coal that might have spilled out of the transports going to the front. They scavenged in garbage cans for any fragment of food. They tried to get work in the factories. They begged from the newly rich walking the avenues. Some of the wealthy were jaded kings of the armaments industry, which was now producing the most powerful artillery in the world. Others were the arrogant lords of the black market, who had their own clever ways to smuggle in food and raise prices. By 1916 families were trading silver and gold to buy a few pounds of dog meat.

Children tried to help their families. If they were lucky, they chanced upon pet cats that had wandered from home. They would kill the cats, skin them, and tell their mothers that the animals were rabbits. Mothers would be overjoyed to have fresh meat and would ask no questions. Some adventurers tried anything and actually became accustomed to the taste of rats. Elegant recipes for rat meat were said to be tasty. With food as hard as it was to come by, people thought of the future only in terms of what they would do the next day. Just getting to tomorrow was an achievement, and people ate anything to get there.

Meanwhile the British, Germany's primary enemy, were handling their food situation much better. Their achievements with food were perhaps more decisive than their military victories, though the British were having those too. Thousands of tons of wheat were transported by convoy from Canada, Australia, and New Zealand, in vessels that one Oxford don called "floating silos." Huge refrigerator ships brought countless tons of beef and lamb from Argentina and South Africa, Australia and New Zealand. Everyone was fed, and no one starved.

And there was more. The same ships transported countless numbers of spry young men from the Commonwealth—men called "the

young lions"—reinforcements whom Germany could barely imagine. Unless the Germans broke this sequence of events, the British
blockade and the escalating war would go on until Germany died.

Anyone taking a train across Germany would see this death
coming, for the poverty of the once-prosperous nation was overwhelming. The land was grey. The horses were skinny. Often the
fields were worked by forced labor from the conquered territories—
that is, by men from Belgium and France, Poland and Russia—men
who deliberately worked very slowly.

General Ludendorff and his staff had fine wine and fresh bread,
while his men in the field ate fake bread filled with sawdust and
leaves. When politicians criticized him for eating better than his
men, he challenged the critics: He would eat the same food as the
men in the trenches, if the critics in Berlin did the same.

At this the critics went silent.

General Ludendorff did not understand the food shortage.
Somehow he managed to convince himself that the starvation
was caused not by his confiscating the chemicals needed for fertilizer but rather by greedy housewives who were hoarding food. Of
course, the housewives were innocent. Many of the nation's desperate housewives were working all day in cold factories and then
spending up to twelve hours in line every night to get food into
their children's mouths for one more day. They even slept on the
pavement. If fortunate, these women could buy turnips or mysterious meat early the next morning. In many markets, women bought
meat labeled as pork, knowing it was really a stolen dog from the
streets. Most people stopped asking what they were eating.

One day in Berlin, an overworked horse died in the street. Before
it could be carted away, a mob of housewives, thinking perhaps of

their children, descended on the carcass with knives in hand and tore the animal apart, leaving only the bones. An actress from Denmark watched, astonished, as a lovely young woman grabbed a chunk of bleeding horse flesh to her chest and ran away happy.

Ludendorff tried to get his men to invent ways to save food, though most of these methods made people laugh. He passed laws forbidding the feeding of pigeons in the park, and he made it against the law to throw rice at the bride and groom at a wedding, as if these measures would make a difference.

The government passed out cookbooks with turnip recipes, but most of the meals were unappetizing. Turnip soup was remembered as "donkey piss." Turnip jam was compared to crank case oil. People said the goo was barely fit for pigs.

Meanwhile, 4,000 boxcars of meat and vegetables went each day to the armies at the front. And even then, the soldiers barely got enough. The men became gaunt. In basic training, some new recruits fainted during exercises.

As a result of wartime conscription and the scarcity of food, birth rates plunged. Ludendorff became worried about having enough soldiers to fight his next war. And yes, he was already talking about the next war, as if one world war were not enough. He passed edicts to ban contraceptives. He could not accept the idea that a German woman had the right to refuse to bring a child into this miserable world, a world that he was destroying.

Protective mothers appealed to the war resisters' network, where they could obtain maps, passes, and guides to get their sons to the Netherlands, to freedom. Often these same German women, doubting their husbands would return, had furtive affairs with the forced laborers on their farms. The women were miserable and were losing their families. The workers were wretched, torn away from their families too. So they had everything in common, and often they drew close. Alarmed, Ludendorff passed laws forbidding women from having sex with foreign workers. People wondered how Ludendorff's police were to enforce this. Would they hide under people's beds and listen for moans?

General Ludendorff, to improve the situation on the home front, increased the numbers of laborers from conquered territories. Here his agents were ruthless. They had already combed the industrial sectors of Belgium and confiscated what machines they could. They had stolen the machinery of whole factories, leaving them as empty as deserted barns. Now Ludendorff's men were moving in and asserting that these Belgian civilians, inevitably out of work, were criminally idle. There was no work in the empty factories, yet these men were accused of not being willing to work. During the winter of 1916, German agents kidnapped thousands of these men and placed them in open boxcars with no food and no latrines, then shipped them through the night to Germany to work the farms and factories there. Those who protested were sent to rickety shacks called "hell barracks." There the floors were hosed down to make sheets of ice, and prisoners had to sleep on the ice until they changed their minds.

During the war, 230,000 Belgians were sent to Germany and forced into labor, with thousands more from France, Poland, and Russia. When an American engineer in Belgium named Herbert Hoover protested ferociously, the Germans retorted that they were paying salaries to the laborers. But no money was paid, and no money went home. Indeed, thousands of the workers never came home either. One immigrant laborer, an educated man who had read *Uncle Tom's Cabin*, said he would have preferred to be a black slave on an American plantation than a foreign laborer working under Ludendorff in this war.

Foreign workers were not the only miserable captives in Ludendorff's empire. German soldiers were becoming captives too. By 1916 Germany had lost 1,600,000 men in the war, and the number was rising, with legions of battered draftees forced to walk like robots into the maw of their all-consuming monster, this war to end all men.

Indeed the word *robot* was coined right after this war, in 1920, by a Czech dramatist, Karel Capek, in the play *Rossum's Universal Robots*. The word described the new trend of the time: the mass production of willing victims, the thinking slaves who were dying by the millions.

At Verdun at the height of the battle, the average German machine gunner lasted fifteen seconds. Yet men did not complain. This war killed these robot men in legendary numbers and became the most murderous event in history, harsher than the bubonic plague of the 1300s or the repulsive syphilis of the 1500s.

One deputy in the Reichstag, a politician named Hans Peter Hanssen, shook his head over this meaningless conflict. In his memoir, aptly titled *Diary of a Dying Empire*, he wrote, "We win and win, but we win ourselves to death." Multilingual, this deputy examined the Scandinavian press and found that the average Dane, reading his newspapers, was better informed about this murderous war than a top-level German statesman reading confidential releases from Ludendorff's headquarters.

Walter Rathenau, the German industrialist who held a senior position in the German War Ministry, put it well: "We shall be victorious unto Death." Rathenau went further and warned that the war had no purpose, no goal. As he put it to a member of the government, "Do you know what we are fighting for? I do not. And I should be glad if you could tell me." Men like Rathenau and Hanssen found no meaning in these victories, and military experts stumbled when they tried to suggest one.

Before the war, a German painter named Franz Marc had done surrealist paintings of blue and red horses and other remarkable subjects. He led a fine life, mingling with friends like van Gogh, who loved his spirit. Then he volunteered for this war, believing the propaganda that the conflict would sweep away the decadence of modern civilization and bring back something finer.

They soon sent this great painter into the fire of Verdun, where he swiftly came to understand that there was nothing noble being ushered in by this mass extermination. The new German style of war made men into animals in a slaughterhouse. "Everything is flaming suffering," Marc sighed. Before his untimely death, when a piece of shrapnel tore into his brain, he warned of the doom sweeping his once-great land. His friends were animals to be butchered, animals who could not understand their fate. He, better than most of his countrymen, understood that because life was so miserable at Verdun, "Death comes as a savior." Among his last words were these: "This war is one of the most evil things to which we have sacrificed ourselves."

On the battlefields of Europe, more than 1,000,000 sacrificed themselves that year. The horses died, the cities crumbled, the libraries burned. Most often the dead soldiers could not be reached and lay where they fell on the field of battle, crucified on the barbed wire in No Man's Land, arms spread wide, like Roman slaves on crosses. Veteran soldiers in the British trenches swore that the bodies of decomposing Bavarians stank worse than the Prussians, but the point was debated.

A noted British writer, the powerful intellect Siegfried Sassoon, wrote a poem titled "Aftermath," which described this misery:

> Do you remember the rats and the stench
> Of corpses rotting in front of the trench—
> And dawn coming dirty white, and chill with a
>   hopeless rain?
> Do you ever stop and ask, "Is it all going to happen
>   again?"

Sassoon, who had served magnificently and won several medals, said he was "finished with the war" and wrote a defiant letter that a friend in Parliament read to a startled House of Lords. He warned people that they could not ask a boy to be the last fellow to die in a mad war. Soon he wrote several inspired works that were anthems for the nation's doomed men, men who were not grateful to be called "the grateful dead"—which was what nations wrote on their war memorials.

A nineteen-year-old boy, Private Elton Macklin from Lewiston, New York, not far from Niagara Falls, wrote about what he saw as a dispatch runner, taking messages all over the battlefield on what chums called "suicide duty." He wrote: "Have you ever watched gut-shot horses, screaming, dragging his shell-killed mate, his dead driver and his wagon down a bit of road before he dies? Horses die more noisily than men." Macklin wrote a witty memoir titled *Suddenly We Didn't Want to Die*, which sold well. Even though he and others runners belonged to the "suicide squad," he got through the war in fine form.

But few were so lucky. Death pursued almost everyone. Even the finest pilot in Germany, Baron Manfred von Richthofen, the famed "Red Baron," was known to mutter that some day it would catch up with him. And of course he was right. A single stray bullet hit him on a reconnaissance flight.

Men under these mad pressures collapsed frequently. Many went crazy. Sometimes doctors called the affliction shell shock, sometimes battle fatigue, and often those so afflicted were misunderstood and even shot for cowardice.

General Ludendorff worked magnificently hard, amassing repeated victories but at a cost of pure agony. He was the best soldier in tactics and the worst fool in strategy that most men had seen. In matters of tactics, his skill at maneuvering troops to achieve victory was without equal, and his attention to detail was legendary. But when it came to following a broader strategy and understanding international diplomacy and the national will of different nations, he was abysmal. His military philosophy was based on fighting forever until all enemies died. All in all, he offered only an endless war.

In France, two ace officers, General Edmond Buat and Colonel Georges Becker, did separate studies on Ludendorff, and their acidic conclusions were more useful and more severe than anything published in the English-speaking nations.

First, these officers despised Ludendorff for his endless pretense that Germany was innocent and fighting savage enemies. Buat noted, "The insincerity of Ludendorff is flagrant." Ludendorff despised all adversaries as aggressors and idiots.

Second, they noted in particular that Ludendorff damaged his armies by forcing his plans according to a solid, clear formula. He would write out an overly detailed plan and then assume that his men could do the impossible. He would assume also that the enemy would be inept and incompetent. All in all, he thought his men gods, his enemy devils. He gave his men perfect orders with endless details but never taught them to adapt when the plan broke down. He could never walk into the ring like a gladiator and improvise strategy the way Napoleon could.

Third, he never integrated his offensives. The issue is not how to do endless death; the issue is how to bring it all together to create the end of an otherwise endless war.

Fourth, in war a general must win using his "mass of maneuver." Ludendorff tended to use up this reserve and then moan that he was not supported sufficiently. Alas, he used up his reserves the way a gambler used up his family fortune. And eventually he ran out of men entirely.

Fifth, in war a general must read the enemy's mind and ability. But Ludendorff, who wanted to orchestrate everything, usually wanted to prepare all, without any adaption by the men. Worse, he had no overall vision. Like US generals in Vietnam, he counted prisoners and dead, as if this were a cosmic scorecard. If these numbers were high, he was ecstatic. Never could Ludendorff do what was required of a great general: He did not know how to impose his will on the enemy, win a battle decisively, and then engineer a viable and realistic peace.

Historians have not seen Ludendorff for all that he was, and this is hardly their fault. There was not sufficient access to many historical records until the explosion of the Internet. Only recently has it become possible to make a calm estimate of this man. In truth he was an awesomely confused but powerful man—like the Kaiser, and like Hitler.

His weaknesses were legion. He could not withstand strain; he did not make accurate estimates of enemy armies, especially the American forces, nor of enemy weapons, especially the British tanks; he did not have the ability to see how miserable his own men were, nor how low their morale by 1918, and how little they believed in victory by that last year; he did not learn from errors and above all did not learn from defeat; finally, he did not show an interest in the political or diplomatic dimensions of war, and this would become the most severe threat to him and his army.

First-rate minds have noted that Ludendorff was prisoner of his own propaganda. He ground out so much dreamlike propaganda, tales of great achievements and sacrifice, and an endless vista of German empire and power that he destabilized himself. He also destabilized his elites back home, feeding their greeds, stoking their mental fires. He thus helped turn his army and government into a madhouse, which could only implode and collapse. Finally, Ludendorff never criticized himself or wondered if he were wrong. When all collapsed upon him, like Samson in the temple, Ludendorff only raged that the government and people had not supported him enough. This was rot. The ace German general Wilhelm Groener defended the Germans against this lie: "It would be the greatest injustice to defame the German people for their collapse at the end of the lost World War. They had sacrificed their youth on the battle fields. They had proven themselves . . . in unrelenting work, in privations and sufferings in the homeland. . . . In the end the blame . . . rests on the military."

Ludendorff never saw this. Through the war, until the last days, he never doubted himself. He loved war, continual war, and like the Roman god Saturn, he devoured his sons. His weary wife,

Margarethe, who would eventually lose two of her three sons in Ludendorff's campaigns, was staggered by what her life had become and by what her husband did to her. By 1916 two of the three boys were officers in aviation, risking their lives every morning against the ace fighters of England and France. This was chilling because the new Allied planes were faster, climbed higher, and had powerful engines that dazzled the Germans. There were more Allied planes than German planes, and Allied pilots had more training and came in greater numbers.

The German pilots were doomed—most lasted just days. The Ludendorff boys would go up into the air expecting to be killed, and when they returned alive, they would be relieved. One of them often muttered an exultation, without sarcasm: "I have another twenty-four hours to live!" Mothers with sons in that air force knew what to expect. Some day soon the letters they sent would be returned, stamped with the word "deceased."

Ludendorff kept fighting, without an objective, in an orgy of blood. He did not change an iota of his strategy. Eventually the commander in chief of the Allied forces, Ferdinand Foch, would stop and ask: "Does Ludendorff know his profession?" Foch saw that Ludendorff had a powerful army that he sent forth without a goal or purpose.

Ludendorff convinced himself that he and his officers were the state and that they made all decisions. As a result he took advice from no one. And because he had convinced himself that the German Army was superior, he felt in his bones that they had to win. He had made sure every detail was in place, so how could they fail? And if they were going to win, then why should he take instructions from anyone else?

Ludendorff felt that he was the legitimate ruler of Germany. Essentially he was running a silent coup. Although the German constitution said the Kaiser was supreme, Ludendorff had stolen all power, like a thief in the night. The Kaiser was never the warrior he wanted to be and often was merely a privileged observer. Every time there was a difference between Ludendorff and the Kaiser, Ludendorff would threaten to resign, and the Kaiser would collapse like a straw man.

During this time, the Kaiser went through many ups and downs. In theory he should have been happier, for Ludendorff and Hindenburg reported only the most positive things. But the Kaiser was never told anything at the planning stage. He heard things after they happened, and only if they were favorable. There would be pleasant news about the birth of a zebra calf at the zoo or the building of a veterans' fountain in the park. There would be brief news about the heroic exploit of one soldier who had captured a dozen Frenchmen or a machine-gunner who had killed an entire squad of Englishmen. The generals would give the Kaiser any tidbit to appease him.

To a degree the Kaiser realized this. He once complained, "The General Staff tells me nothing about the war, and never asks my advice. If people in Germany think I am Supreme Commander, they are grossly mistaken." Did he realize how much he had failed? One thing is sure: He had let this happen. Now he cut wood, brooded, drank tea, and read novels. On especially rotten days he blamed the English, then the Jews, and he even urged that people carry out pogroms, "in the Russian fashion."

This has been examined deeply by Professor John C. G. Röhl in his three-volume study titled *The Kaiser and His Court*, published in England by Cambridge University Press in 1994. The last chapter, "Kaiser Wilhelm II and German Anti-Semitism," shows how deeply men like the Kaiser wanted to blame the Jews for what he and his class were doing to their dying nation.

So the Kaiser dithered, and Ludendorff persisted, and the casualties increased. Whatever one might say about Ludendorff, about his poison gases, his enhanced artillery, and his barbed wire, the fact remains that he was the most precise officer in a nation of precise people. As the war went on he became cold, distant, and somehow less than human. A portrait painter named Hugo Vogel confessed to the general's wife, "Your husband gives me shivers down my spine."

Ludendorff laughed rarely. The times he did laugh were when he talked about how American soldiers were worthless mongrels. According to his calculations, the US Army was a tiny force, ranked seventeenth in the world, just after the army of Iran. He was convinced they were of no consequence. He despised them. In similar fashion other officers, like the top admiral of the German Navy, Alfred von Tirpitz, declared the US Army to be "a military zero."

It was a pity for Germany that none of their military leaders seemed to have studied the moment in the American Revolution when Washington had attacked the German mercenaries at Trenton, on Christmas Eve of 1776. That night the Americans smashed a German army and took 900 prisoners, suffering only two casualties in what was the first total victory of the American Revolution. It showed what Americans could do against Germans and suggested how thoroughly the Germans might want to respect the US Army. But the only German of importance in the World War I era who seemed to understand this was their ambassador to the United States, Count von Bernstorff. And people laughed at him when he talked about how impressive Americans really were—so much that he finally would give up on Germany and live in exile.

Ludendorff never listened to men like Bernstorff. "I don't give two hoots for the American Army," he declared. The threat of fighting Americans did not faze him. He said that Americans would not volunteer in large numbers. And if they did volunteer, they could not be trained fast enough. And if they were trained, they could not get to Europe because they did not have enough boats to move everyone. And if there were enough boats, then the German subs would sink them. Ludendorff believed Admiral von Tirpitz, who promised, "I give my word as an officer that not one American will land on the Continent."

But Tirpitz would not be able to keep his word. In fact, more than 1,500,000 Americans would fight on European soil by 1918. Count von Bernstorff tried hard to convince the generals that he knew the United States intimately and that he knew its resources to be "limitless," but Ludendorff would not heed. He laughed at the idea that Americans might build a professional army.

Extraordinarily, Ludendorff's aides further assured him that the German immigrants in places like Milwaukee would revolt and would never allow the United States to make war on their beloved Germany. These aides did not know that liberal Germans had gone to America to escape the right-wing Junkers of the old country and that these people would gladly fight those rabid conservatives and would defend the United States any day of the year.

Astonishingly, millions of German dead from this war did not deter Ludendorff. The pain of this war, the endless losses, did not register. Often he did not really know the depth of the pain. He would never have understood the mind of US general George C. Marshall, who, in another world war, always had casualty numbers typed in red, so he could be reminded what they represented. General Ludendorff was not reminded. He was usually kept away from the front. And when he was near the front, he was surrounded by sycophants, insisting he be kept safe. He and Hindenburg were never under fire. He was never seen talking to a battered soldier anywhere near the front. He never learned what it was like for a soldier to try to sleep in his gas mask, to be unable to wash, to be deprived of toilet paper, to be lacking a toothbrush, to be lacking a fork and having to eat cold food with his fingers, and to be afraid to make friends with a new arrival because the fellow might die the next week, leaving him even more miserable.

Worse, Ludendorff never learned how a German soldier felt when he saw a ten-ton British tank lumbering toward him, his bullets bouncing off like pebbles. Even when sons of Ludendorff's colleagues died, in unnecessary acts for which he alone was responsible, it did not challenge his resolve.

Death like this did not mark him as it marked Rudyard Kipling, the famous English writer. Kipling was devastated by the loss of his boy, Jack, who disappeared in the Battle of Loos, the largest British offensive on the western front in the year 1915. After that battle, Kipling spent years searching for the boy's grave, for details of his death, and for clues about what it meant. He heard a rumor that the lad had died by enemy fire while telling a joke, and he begged to know, "What was the joke?" He wrote haunted lines about his son: "Have you news of my boy Jack? / When d'you think he'll come back? / Has anyone else heard word of him?" But no one heard word of him.

Kipling wrote letters and frantic screeds. He arranged for thousands of leaflets, describing the boy and speculating that the lad might be a prisoner, to rain down on nearby German trenches. He wrote the US ambassador in Berlin and to his friend Theodore Roosevelt in America, for any advice, any clue. Roosevelt, a war veteran of renown who had lost friends in battles he had led, and who would soon lose a beloved son in this war, wrote back a compassionate letter saying, "There are so many things worse than death."

Some soldiers told Kipling that on the second day of the Battle of Loos, Jack had his first moment under fire and was butchered in minutes, like a lamb in a slaughterhouse, his face so mangled that friends barely recognized him. Dead boys, missing sons—there were thousands now, lost in far-off battles and in distant graves.

Lovers of Kipling made it a challenge over the years to find the grave of this lost hero. Three-quarters of a century after the war, in 1992, researchers speculated that Jack was buried at Loos, at a spot in a cemetery noted as Plot 7, Row D. But no one is sure. And how could they be? There were so many bodies blasted about, scattered by artillery, ensconced in the mud or thrown into low-lying pools, with active poison gas still upon them, too dangerous to approach. The authorities found it safer to plow them under, erect a cross, and leave. The crosses bore the abbreviation RIP, and friends suggested that the letters meant "Rise if possible." Kipling wrote scathing lines about the death of these boys in the Great War. He imagined that they were calling out from the grave, saying: "If any question why we died / Tell them, Because our fathers lied."

The losses hurt civilized people like Kipling enormously, but Ludendorff took losses calmly. Only later, when the pressure of leading this war worsened and he began to suspect that it really could be lost, would his wife see just a few changes. She would view him at luncheon, surrounded by officers, discussing reverses, and he would roll his bread into balls. This meant that he was annoyed—with his staff or with the Kaiser, with the home front or with the diplomats, with his allies or with his enemies. But never did this man seem annoyed with himself, because he never blamed himself. This was a trait he shared with the Kaiser—and with his future friend Hitler. These three would rather commit suicide than admit they had erred. It was easier to imagine that the nation had failed them than the other way around.

For him, the horror of war did not exist. To Ludendorff war was man's natural state. Wartime destruction did not upset him because it was the proper course of events. Unlike other soldiers, he did not hunger for peace. For him peace was a bothersome interval between the wonderful years of war. And war, to be good, had to be total. To have the old kind of war, a limited war, a gentleman's war, was to shirk one's responsibilities. Indeed it was to be disloyal.

Ludendorff turned the view of Carl von Clausewitz, the earlier Prussian military strategist who stressed the political aspects of war, on its ear. Clausewitz believed that war is the continuation of politics by other means. For Clausewitz, politics were the central entity. Ludendorff felt that this, in the new age of war, was very much wrong. In his vision, war was the central entity, and politics were merely an extension of war. War to Ludendorff was the major theme of life. Politics and politicians were there to serve the war, nothing more.

This meant that any patriot should strive to produce a warrior state that the nation would serve. It was a savage belief. But it was not foreign to the German soil where it was being sown. One tough

German had predicted it three decades before. Friedrich Engels, the caustic comrade of Karl Marx, put it brutally in a passage written in 1887 that is chilling in its clairvoyance. He predicted where German culture was taking the nation:

> And finally, Germany can no longer fight any war but a World War; and a war of hitherto unknown dimensions and ferocity. Eight to ten million soldiers will strangle each other and in the process decimate Europe as no swarm of locusts ever did. The ravages of the Thirty Years' War telescoped into three or four years and extended to the entire Continent: famine, pestilence, and the barbarization of all armies and peoples . . . ending in bankruptcy, the collapse of the old state, and traditional statecraft . . . to such an extent that dozens of royal crowns will roll in the streets, and no one will want to pick them up.

And Ludendorff led others to think this way. Later he would write a treatise titled "Total War," which Nazis would read with interest. He wanted a war in which the army dominated not only the government but also the churches, so that the nation would have the power to overwhelm all neighboring states. In his view, every man should know how to command or obey.

To a degree Ludendorff was merely a product of this long cultural development. But he held this power. He summed it up, amplified it, brought it together, made it grow, made it glow, and threw it back to the German elites, making it even more intoxicating for them. The problem was that he and his kind would never see that this would demand more of Germany than its people could deliver.

Was there ever another general like Ludendorff? Once, to conceal the strategic movement of artillery at night, he put boxes of frogs on the caissons. The croaking of the frogs masked the sound of the moving artillery, and when his men attacked at dawn, he achieved total surprise. There was no one so clever in matters like these.

Another time, when he was facing a combined force of British and French troops, he hit the hinge between the two armies, for he suspected that here he might find the weakest point.

In addition he sought out clever subordinates, like a colonel named Georg Bruchmüller, a gutsy artillerist who had important new ideas and who was sometimes called the father of modern artillery. He was also known as "the Steamroller." Though he was merely the son of a salesman, and though he was so clumsy that he partly crippled himself while riding a horse, this introspective thinker developed explosive new tactics that could overwhelm an unsuspecting enemy. Bruchmüller insisted on the need for surprise; on the idea that attacks had to be sudden; on having everything concentrated; on targeting the enemy at his command posts, phone lines, and gun positions; and on the artillery's unloading a barrage of fire that would creep forward just ahead of the men. The result was so deadly that his men called his attacks "steel wind."

Georg Bruchmüller's approach became the most efficient way to advance in trench war up to that point, and for this he earned another nickname, Mr. Breakthrough.

So in narrow matters of tactics, Ludendorff was unsurpassed, and he helped Germany endure a two-front war even though it had fewer men and fewer supplies than its enemies. And he did this for years. This accomplishment was major. But in matters of broader diplomatic strategy and international relations, matters that could decide the war, Ludendorff was worse than a country lout. On these momentous issues, when the life of Germany was at stake, he had no vision. He actually believed that one could coax Mexicans into attacking Texas, or that one could coax African Americans to shatter the United States into fragments, or that Germans in Milwaukee would fight against the American people. His only strategy was military strategy, and even that never went beyond the level of battle tactics. "We make a hole and victory will take care of itself," he said vaguely.

But when his troops did manage to rush forward and make a hole in enemy forces, they encountered a brutal problem. As Dr. Kenneth T. Jackson of Columbia University would explain it, the enemy inevitably had some reserves of troops ready for this, all rested, now rushing in by train and truck to plug the gap. This "mass of maneuver" was almost always strong enough to kill the intruding troops. This happened again and again, through most of the war. If by heroism the invading soldiers moved forward a short distance, say several hundred yards, they would make a bulge in the line, and the defending troops could then butcher the Germans from several different angles. The invading Germans, shredded on three sides, would reel back, having lost countless men, and the stalemate would continue. Jackson, one of the stars of the Columbia University History Department and the president of the New York Historical Society, is adamant that this dilemma was a major reason the war became an eternal stalemate.

War had changed. As the esteemed historian Robert L. O'Connell has noted, the Germans continued to talk about Cannae and Hannibal. Indeed, the German Army theorists would keep chattering about Cannae until the next war. But war had deviated from the old forms. A general now had to analyze the results of each move, the interconnecting implications and ramifications that bounced off each other like billiard balls on a cosmic plain.

Some had seen the shift coming. Some had studied the American Civil War, which had started as a fast-moving war with cavalry charges and bayonet attacks over open fields, at places like Bull Run in 1861; and then had slowed down to a series of slugging matches, like Gettysburg in 1863; and finally had been frozen into endless, plodding trench war, like the defenses outside Richmond in 1865. Clearly something was evolving—but to what?

A genius in Warsaw, a Jewish economist named Jean de Bloch, wrote a 3,000-page prediction about this new kind of conflict titled *The Future of War,* which was published in 1899 and reprinted many times after. As Bloch saw it, the new rules of war had changed life on Earth. He said you could look back and esteem George Washington, who won his Revolutionary War with 7,000 battlefield deaths, but such a modest price of victory could not occur again. In this new world of war, a nation could lose 300,000 men in the first days of hostilities, as the French did in the first summer of the Great War, and this would be but the beginning.

The old wars of the past, in a famous phrase from the French poet François Villon in the Middle Ages, were "gone with the wind." Bloch counseled one and all that with railways and artillery, with barbed wire and machine guns, with dreadnought destroyers and the new airplanes, any conflict would degenerate into a desperate war that would involve 1,000,000-man armies, gigantic casualties, and endless butchery. This new war would bring famine and bankruptcy and would wipe out dynasties.

Bloch went further. He said that the new artillery pieces would be "mutually exterminating." Unless one outnumbered the enemy by at least eight to one, a large-scale attack would fail. Kipling's son died miserably at the great defeat at Loos in 1915 when the British had an advantage of seven to one. And many more British sons would die from poison gas—their masks did not work well, the new lenses fogged up, and so they took them off and died. Guts went far but not far enough.

And then came starvation. You could not feed gigantic armies in the field *and* the people at home. You had to choose. Inevitably a general like Ludendorff would feed his army. But soon starving people at home wrote lonely letters to the boys in the trenches, telling them how miserable everyone was. This destroyed the morale of many a young man.

So it was that once happy people stumbled through the war like zombies. Famed explorer Sir Ernest Henry Shackleton spent more than a year at the South Pole and came back to the outside world in 1916. He asked the first person he met, "When did the war end?" The answer chilled him: "The war never ended," a friend replied. "Europe has gone mad."

The changes that came with the war crept into language. Civilians talked of men being "over the top," a phrase that originated with soldiers climbing out of trenches. If a man were evil, civilians called him "lousy," a term that first described soldiers afflicted with lice. A man who was incapable of something was called a "basket case," allegedly the way soldiers described a man with no arms or legs, who had to be put in a basket.

The brutality of the war extended into every crevice of life, and the elegant limited war, the way war was done by gentlemen, was

LUDENDORFF ATTACKS IN 1916

forgotten. Instead men now used the phrase coined by General Grant in the midst of the American Civil War. In Virginia in the spring of 1864, Grant described how he would defeat the South: "I determined to hammer continuously against the armed forces of the enemy and his resources, until by mere attrition the military power of the Rebellion was entirely broken."

Europeans rarely studied war of attrition as practiced by Grant. Indeed the brilliant *Oxford English Dictionary* is surprisingly ignorant and dates the term *war of attrition* only to a 1914 article in the *London Times*. If Europeans had studied American history in depth, they might have been less amazed how devastating the new war could be. In a world war, attrition comes like the apocalypse. It overwhelms everyone and reduces life to daily horror.

Only a few liked this new kind of war. At the Battle of the Somme, a weird Austrian soldier of the Sixth Bavarian Reserve Division got a bullet in the leg and was proud of the medal he earned there. He had never succeeded in life until then, and he was ecstatic to do well in this war. His name was Adolf Hitler, and he was one of those few who believed this war brought glory to Germany.

But the war brought only deadlock and slaughter. Interesting to report, one Allied general managed to figure out how to launch a successful offensive. General Aleksei Brusilov, probably the best officer in the Russian Army, saw that the Austrians were the weak link in the German chain, and he decided that he would shatter that link. In June 1916 he hit their army with multiple surprises. He delivered a short artillery barrage, so short that the enemy did not have time to react. Then along a wide stretch of front he hit the Austrians with separate units of shock troops, small units that each assaulted a specific vulnerable point. The Russian troops advanced, bypassing every strong point and streaming into the rear, shooting the cooks and clerks and generals and sowing confusion so vast that the Austrians had no time to regain their balance or launch a counterattack.

The Russian casualties were severe, but they were victorious. The Austrians lost 1,325,000 and were never again a valid force in World War I. The attack was named the Brusilov Offensive and was the only successful Allied advance named after a general. Winston Churchill applauded the Russian's "blood, toil, tears and sweat"— a thundering phrase that he would use famously later, somehow misquoted as "blood, sweat, and tears." Churchill praised Brusilov to the skies. In Churchill's book on the Russian Front called *The Unknown War*, he celebrated Brusilov above all other Russian generals.

But the genius of Brusilov backfired. For once Ludendorff studied an enemy victory quickly and learned its lessons. Soon he would unleash the same tactics against the French and British, with terrifying results. Ludendorff persevered, worked hard, and let no bad news sink him. Indeed he worked too hard—in four years of war, he took only three days of leave. His health began to suffer, he now drank, and he developed a severe exophthalmic goiter, a nasty thyroid condition that makes the eyes bulge and the thyroid malfunction. With passion he lurched toward destruction and forced Europe into an orgy of ruin that would set the continent back, in its population levels and in its economy, for years to come. Nothing stopped him and his generals, for they had convinced themselves that they could win this barbarous war if they merely increased the savage fighting until no enemy could stand it. He had no way to know that the allegedly decadent democracies such as England, France, and the United States were stronger than Germany ever could be, and that they could fight longer. Indeed he was condemning Germany to war and ruin.

Edward M. House, representative of the American president Woodrow Wilson, came to Germany during this war and was shocked to find that many top German leaders thought like Ludendorff and had the same myopia. They were convinced that it would come out right in the end. House met but one German official who saw through this, and that man was the industrialist Walter Rathenau.

Rathenau was a thinker, descended from one of the great rabbis in Barcelona in the Middle Ages, a man who spoke the truth to a nation that avoided inconvenient truths. Rathenau wanted the war to end when few Germans realized how easily they could do this. He understood, and Churchill in England stated later, that all the Germans had to do was call for a peace based on no annexations and no indemnities. People would stop fighting and go home.

This would almost certainly have worked. But instead Ludendorff launched a propaganda offensive over Germany, preparing the people for more battles. He created two new policies. One was the Hindenburg Program, calling for a huge increase in arms and manpower. The other was the Ludendorff Peace, which, despite its name, called for a ruthless escalation of the war to force a victor's peace via the battlefield.

In the first program Ludendorff wanted a doubling of ammunition and mortars and a tripling in artillery and machine guns, plus vast quantities of aircraft, antiaircraft guns, and poison shells and thousands of miles of barbed wire. The only thing he did *not* want was tanks, those newfangled weapons invented by the British, which bored Ludendorff and which he refused to study. How, he wondered, could clumsy machines, some of which moved a mere five miles an hour, make a difference?

As he would later discover, the British invention of the tank, using the caterpillar treads invented in America for tractors, was the best new idea in the war. In far-off California, people like Benjamin Holt of the Holt Tractors Development Company had suggested that the army encase its tractors in armor, and eventually the British agreed.

Ludendorff's plans to win the war became more extreme as the war went along, and he forced people to his views. He changed the laws of Germany so he could punish slackers. He made every male between twenty and fifty subject to forced labor. He ordered every housewife to go to the forest and get extra herbs for her family's salads. He flooded homes with cheerful pamphlets describing the future that was in store after he won the war. He also threatened any women on the home front who spread defeatism. This is to say, it was a crime to note that Germany was losing the war.

Ludendorff also began to make multiple promises about a massive victory that would change the world, with stupendous gains for Germany and its allies. Lectures, films, and books testified to this vision. "Times are difficult but victory is certain," ran the slogan.

The propaganda by Ludendorff indicated that he intended to win total victory, in the West *and* in the East. General Ludendorff was demanding the world. At a time when at least a few German generals were advocating a modest victory for Germany, one that would offer a lasting peace and would not make France and Russia enemies forever, Ludendorff demanded ten victories:

(1) Germany would get Belgium;

(2) Germany would get the French coast from Calais to Dunkirk;

(3) Germany would get the Channel Islands from England;

(4) Germany would get the Belfort fortress and the Longwy-Briey ore fields in France;

(5) Germany would get Estonia, Latvia, and Lithuania;

(6) Germany would get the French and Belgian colonies in Africa, including Congo, a land larger than Texas;

(7) Austria would get vast territory in Poland;

(8) Austria would get Ukraine;

(9) Austria would get Egypt; and finally,

(10) Germany and Austria would get vast indemnities to pay the cost of the war.

As a Spanish king would say, "The world is not enough."

These demands intoxicated many people and lessened some of the pain creeping over the land during the Turnip Winter, when so many starved. And, unbelievably, some elites soon decided that they wanted *more* than Ludendorff's demands. These were Pan-Germans, Army Leaguers, and Navy Leaguers who felt that once the Germans were victorious, they should also demand colossal chunks of Romania and Serbia. On certain days there were additional demands about getting parts of Holland, France, and Finland.

Ludendorff soon started to talk about getting Madagascar, Tahiti, Tsingtao, and Valona, some of which were so obscure that even a trained diplomat might not know them. Valona, for example, is an obscure stretch on the coast of Albania.

Some elites also dreamed of taking huge swathes of the French and British empires in Asia and beyond, like Vietnam and India. The wild dream of India took hold of Ludendorff's fevered brain, and soon it seemed to take on a life of its own. Ludendorff played with the idea that after winning the war in Europe, he would send his troops to take India, the "jewel in the crown," as Benjamin Disraeli called it, and thus give Germany an empire that even Englishmen would envy. But this was folly. How could a man storm India? When a Russian czar, Paul I, sent his Cossacks to take India in 1801, this was seen as insane. The czar sent the men off without maps, but he did give them fireworks to impress the natives. He promised that the Cossacks would find "all the riches of India," and he promised, "You will wallow in wealth."

When this farce was begun, Paul's nobles considered it grounds for killing him—which they did. But the elites in Germany in the early 1900s were not as wise as the elites in backward Russia in the early 1800s. Instead they were bewitched by the dream of invading India, and the concept gained ground. These German nobles at Brest wanted the world.

Every time the elites' demands were added up, the list expanded, for the Junkers were *never* satisfied and were ever raising the list of desired conquests. Just what would Germany do with all this land? How could they incorporate these new populations? Indeed, how could a sane nation have such ambitions? Was Woodrow Wilson's aide Edward House correct when he suggested that Germany was deranged and that there was but one clear head in the nation?

Many of these ambitions for plunder began with Ludendorff. He had turned out so many communiqués that raised men's expectations that he not only hypnotized the public but also hypnotized himself. Ludendorff's exhortations had worked hoodoo on everyone. The result was a hallucinatory distortion of reality that was dangerous and, arguably, suicidal.

The distortion made it next to impossible for him and his staff to make rational decisions. But these were not all the reasons for the distortions at hand. Additional damage had been done long before by the German educational system, which for years had drummed into German minds the conviction that God favored Germany and would never let it fail. One German chancellor, Theobald von Bethmann-Hollweg, moaned that he could not go against this posture. He warned his aides that people would react savagely if he ever told them that they would never get a victory big enough to repay them for their sacrifices. Nothing on the planet could repay Germany for what it was losing in the Great War. "I can do nothing about it," the chancellor moaned. "The mentality of our people has been so poisoned by boasting for the last several years that they would probably become frightened if we denied them."

The worst player in this tragicomedy was the Kaiser. The aide to President Wilson, Colonel House, discussed various matters with the Kaiser but had a difficult time taking him seriously. "His whole attitude was that the War was a royal sport. He told [the American ambassador] Gerard he knew Germany was right because God was on their side, and God would not be with them if they were wrong.

And it was because God was with them they had been enabled to win their victories."

House wondered if the Kaiser were posturing or insane.

So the German military hypnotized themselves into believing that the German Army could not fail because it was perfect, and the superpatriots convinced themselves that the German nation could not fail because God loved it. Together these groups were gloriously confident as they rushed to destruction.

And so it was that the Kaiser, the educators, and Ludendorff turned away from the tolerable peace they could have had in 1916, after which their superior industrial capacity might have won them an empire in the world of business, and instead went for a total military victory: a victory that would conquer the world, a victory they saw as inevitable, but a victory that was impossible.

CHAPTER 5

Ludendorff Begins His Five Great Campaigns

S ENSING THAT HE would not win all his decisive victories soon
enough on the battlefield, Ludendorff turned to the German
Foreign Office to try other maneuvers to advance Germany's cause.
His ally there was a kindred spirit named Arthur Zimmermann, the
current undersecretary of state. A fifty-year-old who was said to con-
sume a bottle of Mosel wine every day at noon, Zimmermann was a
big ruddy bachelor with a bushy moustache and a dueling scar. He
was the kind of adventurous German whom Ludendorff would find
sympathetic, a brash middle-class outsider like Ludendorff himself.
Together he and Ludendorff tried five startling new campaigns that
they hoped might win the war in months.

THE FIRST CAMPAIGN
Ludendorff and Zimmermann Attack the British in India

Ludendorff knew that the British Empire was formidable and that
their colony in India was their "jewel in the crown." Together he
and Zimmerman hatched a plan to send arms from California to
India in an American ship called the *Annie Larsen* to seize the jewel

and destroy the crown. The ship was a fragile schooner built in 1881 that hardly looked like an effective weapon. Ludendorff and Zimmermann put together a shipment of 4,500 rifles and 4,750,000 cartridges to deliver to rebels in far-away India.

British spymasters learned of this plan and informed the Americans. The Americans seized the ship and put the conspirators on trial in San Francisco in a frenzy that made headlines all over the world.

When details of the plot came out, military observers were astonished at Ludendorff's incompetence, for they determined that the ship was not capable of carrying such a heavy cargo. It could never have reached India. Also, the ship was not staffed with a loyal crew. The Germans and Indians recruited into this conspiracy were unreliable.

The trial in San Francisco began on November 12, 1917, and went into the next year, through April 24, 1918. During this time, a total of 105 people were put on trial, and there were rascals giving testimony against one another in six languages. There were nine Germans, seventeen Hindus and Sikhs, and many more sailors of exotic origins, all screaming and giving different testimonies. The prosecution brought in the German consul under subpoena, several revolutionaries from different parts of India, and at least one double agent.

The process got complicated the last day, when one defendant pulled out a pistol and killed another and then wounded the US marshal, an expert shot who returned fire. All three died.

When experts examined the equipment in the hold of the *Annie Larsen*, they found that the bullets were rusty and the vessel was leaking. Almost certainly the ship would not have gotten more than halfway across the Pacific and would have sunk somewhere near

Hawaii. By the time the trial was over, there were two cases of insanity, three of murder, and one of suicide.

And to further embarrass Ludendorff, the British found documents that he and Zimmermann had a sub-plot within this plot. One of the Indian revolutionaries, a Bengali playboy named Dr. Chandra Kant Charravarty, was entrusted by Ludendorff to contact the Chinese government and enlist that new republic to wage war on England, too. The hope was to get the Chinese to bring together all anti-British elements in China, Japan, Java, and Sumatra. Charravarty knew nothing about the revolutionary situation in those lands; he was an over-sexed German-speaking playboy with wild experiences in Berlin and New York. He took a great deal of money from Ludendorff and Zimmermann and went to New York City, where he invested the cash in real estate, a grand new wardrobe, and various sexy women. To all appearances he was extraordinarily pleased with the financial and personal returns this entailed. And his treaty with the Chinese? It was vetoed by the top statesman in China, Sun Yat-sen, who saw the Bengali playboy for the buffoon that he was.

And so died Ludendorff's vision to launch trouble for the British in India and China, Java and Sumatra.

THE SECOND CAMPAIGN
Ludendorff and Zimmermann Plan a Revolt in Ireland

Ludendorff soon developed the idea of collecting all the Irish soldiers he could find, selected from British prisoners of war that Germany had captured on the battlefield, and sending them to Ireland to fight the British for Irish independence. He obtained the

services of a titled Britisher named Sir Roger Casement, a famed
liberal with a distinguished record of launching crusades for the
natives of South America and South Africa. Soon Casement was
touring the prisoner-of-war camps in Germany to find soldiers of
Ireland for what he called a Rebel Brigade.

On paper this plan looked solid. Ludendorff would send
thousands of Irish soldiers back to Ireland to fight against King
and Country. But this plan had problems. Casement had trouble
rallying any prisoners to his cause. He spoke glowingly of the
Rebel Brigade that would fight for the freedom of Ireland, but
his vision was cloudy. There were patriotic men of Ireland in the
British forces, many of whom wanted independence. Some had
complaints against the English. But these Irishmen were decent
fellows, and they were aghast at the German atrocities they had
witnessed in the war. As they saw it, the English errors in Ireland
were nothing compared to the horrific crimes of the Germans in
the world war.

Additionally, the Germans had been treating the Irish soldiers
like dogs in the camps. They were given exhausting work, wretched
food, and terrible punishment if they protested. These Irish lads
wanted nothing to do with Germany.

Besides, every Irishman in a British uniform knew that if he *did*
join the Rebel Brigade, he would be a traitor under British law. His
family, now drawing his salary as a British soldier, would be cut off
and could starve.

When Casement came to the camps to enlist the Irish, they spat
in his face. Prisoners threatened him so severely at one camp that
he found himself sucked into the midst of a human whirlpool and
needed German guards to get free. At one large camp he found

only three Irishmen willing to serve. A few dozen Irishmen in all of Germany joined the ill-fated brigade.

While attempting to recruit these men, Casement could not get Ludendorff and Zimmermann to cooperate fully with the project. The few men joining the brigade were declared to be free and were officially allied to Germany, or so it was said. But the Germans still locked them up every night like prisoners. Even when Ludendorff got them their own uniforms, these Irishmen were still kept in prison like convicts.

Worse, Ludendorff refused Casement's foremost request, that he and Zimmermann send German troops alongside the Irish to help mount the insurrection. Instead the Irish rebels would go in alone. The power of the British Empire would then be turned against these few stalwarts, and they would be butchered. Casement knew that his men would be killed, their names disgraced, their families impoverished.

Casement was so gloomy over his chances that even though he did agree to go to Ireland to launch the revolt, he secretly considered calling it off upon arrival.

Unfortunately for Casement, Ludendorff's planning of this campaign was like that of the *Annie Larsen* escapade. Munitions were not landed, secrecy was not kept, and plots were not concealed. Like a true Don Quixote, Casement went forward anyway, with no army and no ammo. The British captured him and put him on trial for treason. Within days one could read all the details in the London press.

Cleverly, the British released parts of Casement's diary that seemed to prove that he was a homosexual, with all sorts of notations about his couplings with unwilling boys in the dark forests of South America and South Africa. Now disgraced, Casement no longer had anyone's sympathy. People forgot that he had earned a reputation for helping oppressed minorities and had been knighted by the king. He was found guilty of both treason and rape, and when this rebel died, the world rejoiced that British law was killing a rapist and a traitor who was getting what he deserved.

Some apologists have suspected that the British forged the sexual parts of the man's diary, but no one could prove it. Years later, in 2012, the Nobel Prize–winning author Mario Vargas Llosa of Peru published a well-researched 404-page novel about this man, which said that the British forged nothing.

And so died Ludendorff's revolt in Ireland.

THE THIRD CAMPAIGN
Ludendorff and Zimmermann Push Mexico to Invade Texas

Ludendorff's plan to get the Irish to go to war with England was implausible and indeed ridiculous, but it was brilliant in comparison to his next campaign, involving Mexico. Somehow in his feverish and overworked brain, Ludendorff believed he could persuade Mexico to invade the United States of America and overrun the Southwest. Despite the fact that the fragile government of Mexico was in a civil war and was in decline, Ludendorff wanted to convince them to invade the United States and seize the territory from Texas to California.

His plan, mad but fascinating, went this way:

First, Ludendorff and Zimmermann sent a telegram to President Venustiano Carranza of Mexico in a secret code, proposing that "Mexico is to reconquer the lost territories of Texas, New Mexico and Arizona" in the event of war between the United States and Germany. Germany would provide arms and ammunition and would support "any invasion by Mexico of US territory."

This weird communication, known as the Zimmermann Telegram, landed on the desk of President Carranza, and Carranza could not believe his eyes. The Mexican president was already under siege, fighting a losing civil war against the most effective guerrillas in Mexican history—Zapata and Villa. These rebels were formidable adversaries, capable of heroic achievements. When his government was busy losing a civil war with these rebels, why would Carranza wish to attack the United States?

Carranza wondered how Ludendorff could think that he would attack Texas. Texans were famous in Mexico as the toughest gringos in the world, and Mexicans had met them once before, at the Alamo. Further, Carranza's aides pointed out that if they did agree to this scheme, how could Germany, now blockaded by the British, deliver arms to Mexico? And if Mexico did win such a war, how could Mexico absorb the millions of new subjects, much less obtain their loyalty? President Carranza commented, "I would not know if we had annexed them, or if they had annexed us." Carranza felt that Ludendorff was promising help he could not deliver, in a war he could not win.

Worse, Carranza knew his government was collapsing. The corruption of the government was so bad that a great Spanish novelist, Vicente Blasco Ibáñez, called the nation "a cave of thieves." There was even a new verb in the language, *carrancear*, which meant "to steal." Carranza's wife was moving their valuables to a safe house in San Antonio, in case a revolution erupted. There was no way he could accept Ludendorff's scheme.

The scheme, already a farce, soon became a disaster. Though Ludendorff and Zimmermann had dispatched this proposal in a code that they believed to be secure, they underestimated the British, who easily translated the message and leaked it to the president of the United States, Woodrow Wilson, who became enraged. And then the British leaked the news to newspaper editors throughout the United States, and they became even more furious. The reactions were volcanic. The *Buffalo Courier Express* imagined "hordes of Mexicans under German officers sweeping into Texas, New Mexico and Arizona." The *New York American* saw Germany taking the East Coast, enslaving Americans, and exacting indemnities. "Citizens, prepare!" the paper urged. "The hours are short and the days are few."

Ludendorff and his aides were surprised. They thought their codes were secure, and they believed the Mexicans would accept their offer.

Ludendorff's ultimate plan for the United States was to shatter the republic into five balkanized governments. There would be a chunk of Texas and New Mexico run by victorious Mexicans. There would be a republic in the South run by vengeful blacks. There would be a massive area in the Midwest run by triumphant German Americans from Wisconsin. And at the last moment there were amendments to the plan, whereby Ludendorff wanted to give the West Coast to Japan and the East Coast to Germany.

Americans exploded. Teddy Roosevelt called this "the Prussian Invasion Plan" and "a declaration of war." To have enraged Roosevelt was a colossal mistake, for Roosevelt was the most popular man in America. Ludendorff's plan was driving German–US relations to the depths.

Things got worse. The ferocious American reaction, relayed back to Germany so anxiously by the German ambassador in Washington, convinced Ludendorff and Zimmermann that the United States was now their enemy, and so they decided that they should henceforth treat it as such. This in turn pushed Ludendorff and Zimmermann to their fourth campaign, directed squarely against the United States: They decided to unleash the German Navy against all American shipping, so no American goods could get to England. This decision changed the history of the world.

THE FOURTH CAMPAIGN
Ludendorff Launches Unrestricted Submarine Warfare and Brings America into the War

Ludendorff felt that the British were persevering *only* because of the immense supplies they were receiving from the United States and other English-speaking nations. As he saw it, if the German submarines torpedoed all the ships delivering these goods, the Germans could destroy Britain in short order.

Glibly, Ludendorff declared that the United States and Germany were already in a de facto state of war, so Germany lost nothing by attacking American ships and sending them to the bottom of the Atlantic. He was convinced that the German submarines could do that and that with unrestricted submarine warfare, the Germans could win the war in one last push.

It would be a Battle of Annihilation on the high seas.

The naval experts in Berlin gave reassuring estimates, and their numbers were both comforting and confusing. Some naval experts claimed that they could sink 300,000 tons of enemy ships each month; some said 500,000 tons; and some said 600,000 tons. Some experts in Berlin said that with this escalated naval war, England would collapse in two months. Others said six months, and some said twelve months. A real thinker would distrust any aides who gave such wildly varying estimates.

Years later, after Germany lost this horrific war, scholars pored through the archives of the German Navy and were aghast at the vagueness of these life-and-death estimates, on which people were betting the future of their nation. No one asked specific questions like the following: How many long-range submarines would it take to cripple Britain? How many could be on duty at any moment, while others were in port, literally recharging their batteries? How many of the German submarines might be sunk per month? Was good steel available for making replacements? How swiftly could they build replacements? What percentage of German submarines should be long-range submarines, and what percentage should be short-range? These were the questions that the elites should have asked before they bet the life of the nation on his plan.

Yet Ludendorff blithely declared that an unrestricted submarine campaign would win the war. Said he: "It is the only means to secure a victorious end to the war within a reasonable time." In all of Germany, only Walter Rathenau disagreed. He said: "It will not work and it shall bring in the United States."

Two factors contributed to this colossal error. First, Ludendorff was guilty of cherry-picking—that is, taking information that would buttress his case and disregarding all else. Simultaneously his subordinates were guilty of stove-piping—that is, sending to Ludendorff the ideas he wanted to hear and eliminating all else. It was a case of reciprocal brainwashing.

Ludendorff cheerfully went forward with his plans for total submarine war against the Americans. He and his aides convinced one another that the Americans were not important, that they did not have a large army, and that they could not build one quickly. And even if they did, they could not get it to Europe because German submarines would sink them. Ludendorff assured everyone that his plan would work and that the British would collapse.

But the British had what was arguably the best navy in the world, and when the Germans launched unrestricted submarine war, the British answered fiercely. They adopted a convoy system so that the Royal Navy could react the instant a ship was attacked. They also constructed the most lethal depth charges known to man, their murderous 300-pound Type D underwater bombs, which sank any sub within eight yards of a blast. To deliver these, the British invented machines that catapulted them out like pebbles from a child's slingshot.

And there was more. The Royal Air Force discovered that their pilots could see the German submarines from above if the submarines were in clear water. When they could see them, they destroyed them. The British then built several antisubmarine research centers in England, which developed decoys called Q-ships. The sailors on these vessels pretended to be unarmed merchantmen, but when the German subs came near, they opened their hatches and blasted away.

They also developed hydrophones, which allowed the British to analyze the sound of propellers by their frequency and thereby determined which subs were enemies. Soon, even in the dark of night in the North Atlantic, the British could ferret out an enemy submarine. Enemy crews began to moan that the British were turning the Atlantic into a sea of glass.

And there was yet more. British propagandists dropped well-composed leaflets on German submarine pens along the Atlantic coast. The leaflets used published German data to prove that the average sub crew died after four missions. The result was that the German crews were glum on their fifth mission and beyond, for they knew where they were going.

The British also developed curtains of thin steel some 200 yards long with calcium lights on top. The moment a German sub touched a curtain, the lights went on and indicated its presence. Soon the Royal Navy installed 1,000 miles of these curtains, with grave results—indeed resulting in many watery graves.

The British even trained birds to help them! British submarine commanders would drop fish in their wakes so that seabirds became accustomed to finding food near submarines. Eventually these birds would go screaming after any submarine, looking for food, so when a German sub came into British waters, the squawking birds instantly indicated its presence. The British would see the fuss and come in for the kill.

The British made a brilliant maneuver to convince the Americans to join the fight against Ludendorff's forces. Germany's submarine warfare sank the great steamship *Lusitania* off the Irish coast, killing more than one hundred Americans and more than 1,000 other passengers. A German maker of commemorative medals in Munich, a private citizen named Karl Goetz, designed a medal extolling the destruction of this ship. On one side of the medal, Death was selling tickets to fools boarding the vessel. On the other side, the ship, allegedly loaded with munitions, was going down to the bottom of the sea.

Back in England, Lord Newton, head of the propaganda office, examined the medal and saw an opportunity. He employed a great department store, Selfridge, to make 250,000 copies of the medal and sell them for pennies each. With each medal, Selfridge enclosed a paper that declared, "This medal has been struck in Germany with the object of keeping alive in German hearts the recollection of the glorious achievements of the German Navy in deliberately destroying an unarmed passenger ship, together with 1198 non-combatant men, women and children."

Inevitably, people were shocked by the barbarity of the medal. Everyone assumed it was an official medal of the German government, though the British did not claim that this was the case—they simply gave the impression that the medal was official. And eventually Germany's situation, with undeclared submarine warfare and with propaganda like this medal, became dire. Ludendorff had not only failed to defeat England; he had helped it by enraging the Americans, whose ships were sunk and whose citizens were massacred. Within months, the United States had declared war.

Some first-rate historians, like Professor Holger Herwig at the University of Calgary in Alberta, Canada, are convinced that these zany campaigns brought the United States into World War I and that this, in turn, cost Germany the war. Herwig's reasoning is simple. With the power of the United States added to the power of the British Empire, the French Empire, and Russia, there was no way that Germany could win. The resources of Germany's enemies were now stupefying. Herwig notes that when the United States went to war, its government made plans to mobilize 4,000,000 men by 1919. How could Germany defeat such a force?

Ludendorff, now working eighteen hours a day, was becoming irritable. Somewhere in his mind he must have sensed a shift in the balance of forces against him. Between April and July in 1917, Ludendorff put pressure on the Kaiser to sack the current chancellor, Theobald von Bethmann-Hollweg, who had been warning everyone of the consequences of enraging the Americans. In July Ludendorff and Hindenburg threatened to resign if Bethmann-Hollweg were not fired. Predictably, the Kaiser gave in, though he seemed to despise himself for doing so. "Now I may as well abdicate," the man lamented.

Ludendorff's coup was complete—he had all power in his hands and, he thought, the submarine war under his control. But unfortunately, he also had the United States coming against him. And even if Ludendorff took Paris, the French were prepared to fight on from the west of France and wait for the Yanks to arrive. Further, the British were prepared to blockade Germany into starvation, and Germany was coming close to that. Things looked grim.

But to give him credit, Ludendorff now mounted a fifth campaign, a trick so magnificent that it changed the history of the world and the life of just about every person on the planet. He, the archconservative, made an alliance with Vladimir Lenin to launch a revolution in Russia that would shut down the Russian front and win half the war.

CHAPTER 6

Ludendorff Sends Lenin to Shut Down the Russian Front

B Y 1917 SOME of Germany's miscalculations had become clear to Ludendorff. The celebrated Schlieffen Plan had proven to be naive and its four-month timeline unrealistic. Instead of conquering Europe in four months, Germany had become bogged down in a two-front war that had been going on for years. Also, the Germans had brought the Americans into the war, and the earlier dismissal of American military strength was sending chills up the backs of many senior German statesmen. The Zimmermann Telegram and Ludendorff's authorization of submarine attacks on US ships had incited the Americans to declare war, and now they were making plans to raise a stupendous army. In addition, Ludendorff's diversion of national resources to support the military was forcing German civilians to make sacrifices that resulted in pure agony.

Dismayed, Ludendorff sought someone to blame. Rumors were circulated that Jews in the labor unions were keeping Germany from its victories. Stories abounded about Jews staying away from the front and letting gentiles die in their place. A fanatic minister of war, Adolf Wild von Hohenborn, launched an investigation, trying to prove that Jews were cowards and draft dodgers—he called the investigation "the Jewish census." This backfired when the generals discovered that Jews were dying at least at the same rate as Christians. In fact, their record was more than patriotic. Of the 550,000 Jews in Germany, more than 100,000 were serving. Of these, a whopping 78 percent were risking their lives at the front. Of the Jews in service, some 30,000 would be decorated for valor and 13,000 would make the supreme sacrifice.

Embarrassed, the military elites refused to release this report, pretending hypocritically that they were holding it back "to spare Jewish feelings." They floated rumors that the report *had* substantiated their suspicions, although the opposite was true. In 2002, the details came out when the University Press of Kansas published Bryan M. Rigg's 460-page work *Hitler's Jewish Soldiers,* which proved this in detail.

Unchecked, Ludendorff continued to mutter about disloyal Jews, and then he wondered also about the evil done by Masons, Socialists, and Catholics. Other Germans were also worried. There was so much confusion about the battles on both fronts. Despite announcements of victories, the German people were beginning to be skeptical. The German leaders had no plans beyond the hope that endless fighting would make the Allies surrender.

Then, in 1917, amid these fiascoes, Ludendorff came up with a new plan, a brilliant ploy that changed the world for a century to come. Ludendorff decided that he would send a renowned Communist agitator to Russia to start a revolution that would shut down the front and win half the war.

Vladimir Lenin was living in Switzerland in exile after being arrested in Russia for sedition against the czar. Formerly a senior figure in the Russian Social Democratic Labor Party, Lenin was now a prominent Marxist theorist writing for multiple publications. In these writings he encouraged violent insurrection and called for the war to be transformed into a worldwide proletarian revolution.

Before Lenin's years of exile, Lenin's brother had tried to kill the czar in 1887, and the state executed him. After, the members of Lenin's upper-middle-class family had become outcasts in his hometown of Simbirsk. Lenin's schoolteacher, a kindly man named Fyodor Kerensky, had tried to be decent to him. Theirs was a cultured town, where the great poet Pushkin did some of his best work, and many cultured folk felt that this boy's family should not be punished for one wretched son. But there were others who treated the family abominably, and finally they were made so miserable that they had to go.

Lenin studied law and radical politics and was expelled from his university for participating in an anticzarist demonstration. His politics would lead to his exile to Switzerland, where he tried in vain to develop a revolutionary movement. His life in Zurich was modest. He lived off a dark alley near a sausage factory in an apartment that cost twenty dollars a month, a place where the stink rose so high that he kept the windows closed all day long.

During the war, Zurich was home to exiles and artists from all over Europe, and the Zurich police who investigated revolutionaries soon decided that Lenin was not a significant threat. He had no power. The police were more interested in monitoring the actions of the two famous men in town, James Joyce from Ireland and Tristan Tzara from Romania. The years in exile, the world's indifference, the petty squabbles with fellow Communists, and the aging of his body all weighed heavily on Lenin. He was far from being a decisive actor on the world stage.

He tried to avoid distractions from his dreams of revolution. Every day he rode his bicycle to the library and kept his mind sharp. Reportedly, he gave up chess, Mozart, and even sex in order to concentrate his mind and energies, but to no avail. Lenin had no financial backing, no prospects, no patrons. He said of himself and his wife, "I need to earn money or we shall simply starve, really and truly."

But in March 1917, amazing news had come. A revolution had broken out in Russia, and Czar Nicholas II was deposed. Alexander Kerensky, a Liberal-Socialist who happened to be the son of Lenin's former headmaster, had taken power and was building a Western-style democracy, doggedly committed to keeping Russia in the war. Lenin hungered to return and take power. In Russia the Communists did not know how to overthrow Kerensky, a man whose mind Lenin knew intimately. But with Lenin present, the Communists could subvert Kerensky and seize the state.

The problem was that Lenin could not get to Russia. The country was blockaded. The Germans, who were fighting Russia, would not let him through their blockade. And even if he made it past the Germans, the English, allied to Russia, were at the border, helping to maintain security, and they surely would not let a Communist agitator through.

It was at this point in 1917 that Ludendorff decided to use Lenin to break the deadlock of the war. He knew that the Russian Army was suffering gigantic casualties and was politically vulnerable after the fall of the czar. If one added this renowned agitator, Lenin, to the situation, the present government might fall, and Ludendorff's war on Russia would end. Ludendorff could then transfer 1,000,000 troops to the West, where he believed they could win the war before Americans got to Europe in large numbers.

Ludendorff pushed the idea with his friend Arthur Zimmermann, who concurred and then contacted a well-connected Marxist, Alexander Parvus, a Polish/Russian intriguer who in turn approached Lenin himself. Parvus's question was direct: Did Lenin want to get to Russia to ply his trade as a revolutionary?

Lenin did not hesitate. This was a great opportunity—in fact, this was his only opportunity. Lenin requested that he travel in a sealed train—that is, a train with extraterritorial status—and he wanted to be exempt from being searched. That was all he asked. Instantly he was told that these conditions were acceptable to Ludendorff.

From here the maneuver became a whirlwind. Lenin had his wife pack their possessions, which was easy because they owned so little. Their belongings fit into just three baskets, the kind that housewives used for laundry on washday. Into these Lenin put his cup with a broken handle, a little meat and chocolate, his threadbare clothes, a pile of notes on the revolutionary situation, and books with scribbles on every page.

Soon he was ready. But before he went off to make his revolution, Lenin phoned the American Embassy in Switzerland on April 8, 1917. A twenty-four-year-old youth named Allen Dulles came on the line. Lenin asked if he could meet with Dulles and explained that it was urgent—he said he had sensitive information and asked for a get-together. But Dulles declined. He had a date with a beautiful blonde lady.

"Perhaps tomorrow?" Dulles suggested. He had been trying to get this woman for years and was not going to waste that opportunity for a rendezvous with a minor agitator.

"Tomorrow will be too late," Lenin returned. He said he could drop off the material that evening, but Dulles again declined. Dulles did not understand the urgency, and besides, he thought Lenin was a minor player.

Three major Allen Dulles biographers, Peter Grose, Stephen Kinzer, and James Srodes, have studied this conversation, but none can guess what Lenin wanted with Dulles, the future spymaster. Marxists have suggested to the authors that Lenin may have wanted an exit strategy, a way to go to New York City if all else failed. Men as different as Napoleon III and Trotsky found New York to be a lifesaver when things got hot in Europe.

Dulles, who was later fired for incompetence by John Kennedy for botching the situation in Cuba with Castro, regretted for the rest of his life that he had not pursued this contact with Lenin. Whatever Lenin wanted, it remains a mystery.

Early the next morning, Lenin and his fellow revolutionaries went down to the station to board the train that was waiting by Ludendorff's orders. The train was modest, painted green, with second- and third-class coaches only. The entourage sang "La Marseillaise" while a crowd of Russian exiles jeered. The crowd knew Lenin was making a deal with Ludendorff and saw it as insane. They were disgusted that he was allied with the power that was butchering a generation, and they carried banners printed with wrathful statements like *The Kaiser is paying for your trip! German spies! They will hang you! Pigs!* and *How can you do this?*

A friend of Trotsky's came to the platform screaming, "Lenin is out of his mind! Tell him to stop this mad journey!"

Blocks away, the famous writer James Joyce laughed, "Ludendorff must be desperate. Ludendorff–Lenin?" But Joyce observed that Lenin in his sealed train might be an effective Trojan horse. He said that if Lenin and his men got into Saint Petersburg, the city could fall like Troy. In England, meanwhile, Winston Churchill expressed his scorn scathingly and accused the Germans of transporting Lenin like a grisly and poisonous germ from Switzerland to Russia.

The traveling companions whom Lenin had selected were powerful intellects. There was the debonair Karl Radek with his burning eyes, tortoiseshell glasses, and wonderful jokes. He was a deserter from the Austrian Army and the Germans could shoot him if they wished, but he was as blithe as could be. Stalin would kill him in 1939, in circumstances so obscure that it would be decades before anyone would know even the year of that murder. Then there was Lev Kamenev, Lenin's intimate friend, an old-time Communist married to Trotsky's sister. Stalin would kill him in 1936, then kill his sons and wife later. There was Grigory Zinoviev, another intimate, one of the few gentle revolutionaries in this fierce assembly. Stalin would kill him in 1936. And there were others, a mass of devoted Communists, all willing to die for the cause. Ironically, almost all of them would perish for that cause, but not at the hands of the capitalists. They would die at the hands of their own leaders.

From the train window, Lenin addressed his supporters in words of confidence: "Either we shall be swinging from the gallows in three months, or we shall be in power!" A young girl squeezed his hand. Did she know the danger lurking along the way? Socialists sang the workers' hymn, the "Internationale," with its stirring words: "Arise, the workers of all nations! Arise, the oppressed of the earth! For justice thunders condemnation! A better world's in birth!"

And now began one of the most amazing locomotive rides since the day the English invented trains. So much happened during this voyage that an ace writer, Michael Pearson, dedicated a whole book to it. Titled *The Sealed Train*, it showed all the dialogue and detail, plus the risks and rewards, that this anabasis entailed.

As soon as the train lurched forward, everyone began to talk excitedly, smoke cigarettes, and guess what was to come. The smoke became so thick that Lenin had to insist they light up only in the latrine. Alas, this produced an impossibly long line of people waiting for the toilet, only a few of whom really needed to go. If there were a sarcastic philosopher present, he would wonder how well Lenin would be able to organize an effective state if he could not handle a simple matter involving toilets and tobacco.

Lenin looked out to Germany and saw decay. There were few German men to be seen—only underage boys and forced laborers from abroad were out working. Along the way, at one of the stops, some German girls, obviously undernourished, served them pork and potatoes. Lenin generously gave them his portion. In this land of famine, these girls were grateful.

Soon the talk on the train became grim. Lenin tried to guess how many days they had left to live. One part of his mind told him that he was going to lead a revolution that would shake the world, and the other part told him he would die the minute he got there.

The train stopped at the Potsdam station in Berlin in the night. The streets were dim. Lenin saw peasant soldiers on the railway platform, furtively eyeing him and his fellow revolutionaries. The poor fellows asked the travelers when they thought the war might end. The agitators with Lenin turned the question around: "Do you soldiers want to start your own revolution?"

The poor fellows did not answer. Most likely, no one had ever asked their opinions, and they were not accustomed to being treated like people of value.

Then emissaries from German military headquarters came to confer with Lenin. This was a secret session, and to this day, no one knows the names of the delegates or the details of the exchange. The group may have included Ludendorff. The train was parked one mile from Ludendorff's headquarters, so it is possible that Ludendorff attended this meeting. When the delegation arrived, the German members got to the point. They informed Lenin that they would give him 40,000,000 gold marks, or about $100,000,000, to help him end the war in Russia. How he used it was his business, but his clear intent was to overthrow the government and build a workers' state. In turn, their intent was that Lenin would pull Russia out of the war and sign any peace treaty they wanted.

For Lenin, an impoverished revolutionary, this was magic. The once-bankrupt agitator was now a millionaire one hundred times over and could fund a new order the instant he got to Russia.

Immediately Lenin's demeanor changed. Before, he had confessed to his fellow revolutionaries that Russia was so backward that it would have to go through multiple developments before becoming a revolutionary state. But with this funding, Lenin declared to all that he could transform Russia by a ruthless uprising that would begin immediately. He would change history starting now. This was exactly what Ludendorff and his circle wanted to hear.

The sealed train soon left Berlin and sped Lenin and his companions toward the Finnish border, where they would try to enter Russia. But here they knew they might have a problem. The British were manning the checkpoints on the border, and at this checkpoint a British intelligence officer named Harold Gruner knew about Lenin, knew how dangerous he was, and suspected that the authorities in Russia might want to bar him from entering.

A single word from Kerensky would have stopped the train like an artillery shell. But the thirty-six-year-old prime minister declared that Russia was a democracy and that a democracy does not keep its people out. So he gave orders to admit Lenin, and Gruner obeyed.

Lenin and his delegation became animated as the train moved over the last miles from the border to Saint Petersburg amid a maze of lakes, forests, and granite outcroppings. Lenin sat looking out the window, deep in thought.

Then, on the evening of April 16, 1917, at 11:10 PM, Train 293 arrived, a half hour late, at the Finland Station in Saint Petersburg. Lenin looked out, perhaps thinking he would see a mob with a noose, but he saw only a sea of friendly faces with bouquets of roses, illuminated through the mist by searchlights.

The Communist cadres of Saint Petersburg, all 2,000 strong, had organized things well. There were ranks of Communist soldiers and sailors, and there were workers with banners and burning torches. There was a band playing martial music. There was a triumphal arch festooned with red banners. And there was a master of ceremonies, Nicholas Chkheidze, an aristocrat from Georgia who had turned radical.

The crowd lifted Lenin onto their shoulders and carried him into the station. "We are the worthy masters of the future," Lenin whispered. The welcoming committee, headed by Chkheidze, nervously escorted Lenin into the waiting room of the czars. Chkheidze then delivered a formal speech asking Lenin to cooperate in building a greater Russia.

"Comrade Lenin," he said, "in the name of the Soviet and the whole Revolution, we welcome you to Russia. . . . But we consider that the chief task of the revolutionary democracy is to defend our

Revolution against every kind of attack, from the inside and the outside. We believe that what we need is union and the closing of the ranks of everyone inside our democracy. We hope you will join us in striving toward this. Our task is to defend the Revolution. We ask you to pursue these goals with us."

The welcoming committee told him that they now had the freest parliament in the world, the only one where women had the right to vote, where Jews had equal rights for the first time, and which even encouraged a loyal opposition. This was somewhat of an exaggeration—the people in New Zealand gave women the vote in 1883, the Americans gave equal rights to Jews, while the British not only had a loyal opposition but had actually invented the term. Still, the claims were sincere, and considering where Russia had been in its development, its progress was unquestionable.

Lenin looked on impatiently. He even looked at the ceiling. These pleasant sentiments and these moderate Communists bored him. To Lenin it was inconceivable for a moderate Communist to take power in Russia because so many Russians did not understand Communism. Only one Russian in about 1,500 was a Communist at that moment, and Lenin knew that to win, he would be doing some killing.

Lenin idly rearranged his bouquet of flowers, and when it was his time to speak, his tone was different. "Dear comrades, soldiers, sailors and workers!" he began. "I greet in your persons the victory of the Russian Revolution! You are the vanguard of the world proletarian army! The predatory imperialist war is the beginning of a civil war that will sweep Europe. Soon the people of Europe will turn their weapons against the masters who have misused them. The sun of the new revolution is rising. . . . Any day the European system will collapse. . . . Your Revolution has paved the way and opened a new era. Long live the new Revolution!"

Some of the people there were afraid. Chkheidze, who wanted compromise in the revolution, with toleration for all, suspected that Lenin would obliterate any opposition. Lenin did not just dis-approve of humanistic Communism; he saw such a compromise as treason. And this gentleman of the old school, who had become a revolutionary, trembled, for he seemed to suspect the powerful at-tacks that were to come.

His fears were not idle. Soon Lenin would drive him person-ally into exile, to France; he would kill 10,000 of his followers in Georgia; and he would drive 50,000 more to Siberia on other grounds. Chkheidze, devastated, would commit suicide in Paris in 1926, shattered, but not surprised.

Lenin, full of amazing confidence, walked briskly outside and talked to the crowd of adoring Communist troops. Searchlights covered him, banners with gold letters sparkled in the light, the air exploded with shouts of his name, and the band played while people lifted Lenin to the top of an armored car so he could speak some more. He stamped his feet for silence and then declared with the fervor of a prophet that he would give no power to the bour-geoisie, only to the workers. He scorned the democratic republics, he said, because their governments had launched this rabid world war. Lenin declared that Communism promised something better than the slaughters of this conflict. He said Communism promised a new world that would sweep away every monarchy and democ-racy in Europe and beyond and build a finer system.

To men like Lenin, monarchies and democracies were equally unacceptable because they were all counterrevolutionary, as they stood in the way of his new state. "We do not need justice. We need the annihilation of all counter-revolutionaries," he said. Lenin had dreams of exporting his revolution from Russia to Poland and then to France, England, and, unbelievably, all the way to India. He saw his firestorm of Communist uprising sweeping the globe. He felt that he had arrived at the decisive moment in history and wanted to lead his divisions to absolute victory. Soldiers in the crowd sensed his power and threw their hats in the air and cheered.

For the first time in his life, this frail man seemed godlike. In the silver sparkle of the lights, people said that he looked like an apparition that had fallen from the sky. He stood, fists clenched, coat open, and saluted the revolutionary proletariat. "All his life had been a waiting for this moment," wrote Lenin's able biographer Robert Payne.

Some people believed that Lenin might be interested in founding a moral world order. But his credo was, "There is no morality in politics. There is only expediency." People believed he would share power. But he said, "What we want is power! Power that is limited by nothing!" Turning to his men, he exclaimed with passion, "We want a merciless mass terror against all enemies of the Revolution!"

Only one spectator seems to have immediately understood the fullest ramifications of this man's arrival: Sir George Buchanan, the British ambassador to Russia, who swiftly cabled London that a new dark force was emerging in Russia, different from any power previously seen on Earth. This man Lenin, he warned, was not just a man dedicated to the idea of bringing revolution to his country. He was also dedicated "to overthrow all the so-called imperialistic governments" in the world.

Lenin sensed the power, the thrust, and it excited him. They now put him into an armored car and escorted him to a palace, the former home of Mathilde Kschessinska, a ballerina who had been the lover of the czar. Clearly, power was shifting.

And now the financial backing from Ludendorff started streaming in. Berlin transferred his funds to the Bank of Stockholm, which forwarded them to the Bank of Siberia, which soon delivered staggering sums to Lenin. With these millions Lenin began to build a base. Soon Lenin was printing 300,000 free copies of the *Pravda* newspaper every day. A Harvard Communist activist named Jack Reed, with two American assistants, helped with the content, the acerbic Karl Radek helped with the rhetoric, and together they published Bolshevik documents and Russian news in flawless German and several other languages to win the hearts and minds of their erstwhile enemies.

There were protests against Lenin. A mob of wounded men, some without arms, some without legs, surrounded his palace and called him a tyrant paid by German gold. Lenin answered them with a ferocious mob of well-fed, sturdy workers, amply paid with the same German gold.

And now Lenin showed his claws. He sent his agents out on special assignments to sow terror among his enemies: Political enemies were tied to planks and fed into furnaces, to be burned to death. Priests were crucified. Nails were hammered into barrels, and critics were placed inside and rolled downhill. Their screams traveled half a mile.

Lenin's agents gave a special punishment to their more vocal adversaries. They would put a rat inside an iron tube and position the end of the tube on a man's belly while heating the other end with a blowtorch. The frantic rat, now being cooked alive, would eat into the man's gut, struggling to get free. Often the rat would go into the body on one side and emerge on the other.

Sometimes Lenin's people were subtle, going after only those thinkers who threatened Lenin's revolution. But often his assistants were lazy thugs who sought an easy fix. For example, when leaders ordered one commissar to kill 300 political enemies a month, the creature went off to the local hospital each month and selected the weakest 300 patients, knowing that they would be easiest to kill.

Meanwhile Kerensky's provisional government made ready to continue the war. Kerensky was a gentleman of the old school. He knew that Russia was honor-bound by its treaty obligations to continue the fight. He also felt he could not pull Russia out of the conflict because then the Germans would have 1,000,000 extra troops to send to fight in the West, troops who might give Germans their long-awaited victory. If this disaster happened, then there would be nothing to stop Ludendorff from returning to Russia in full power and demanding any peace settlement he wished.

Kerensky felt that continuing the war was the lesser evil. So in July 1917, Kerensky launched Russia's last offensive of the Great War. He had no way to know that the strain of carrying out this offensive would destroy his young government.

The offensive started on July 1, 1917. Using new artillery from Britain and Japan, and led by the one superb general they had left in Russia, Aleksei Brusilov, the exhausted Russian soldiers managed a twenty-mile advance. But then it stalled.

Lenin now unleashed his toughest agents upon the Russian Army. His cadres had infiltrated every rank and were ready. Said historian John W. Wheeler-Bennett, "Bolshevik agents appeared in every division, and the success of their work was only too clear. Regiment after regiment revolted, murdered its officers, and the front was paralyzed."

Brusilov, whose hands were tied when Kerensky abolished the death penalty, could not control all his troops. Mutinies erupted down the line as many soldiers shot their officers and went home. Then the remaining soldiers declared that, from now on, the generals would have to submit orders to a soldiers' vote. But this was often ineffective—by the time the vote was tallied, the situation had changed and the approved orders were useless.

A few units still functioned. The world was awed by the valor of the Battalion of Death, a group of female soldiers led by a gutsy Siberian woman named Maria Bochkareva, whom people abroad hailed as "a Russian Joan of Arc." Her troops were the most loyal of Kerensky's soldiers. But they were only a few, and they all fell back and were slaughtered.

The Russian Army, hit by Ludendorff's artillery on one side and Lenin's propaganda on the other, collapsed. On July 16 the advance stopped. On July 19 the Germans counterattacked and broke through. By July 23 the Russian Army was in fragments. Ludendorff's troops advanced at will, took 42,000 prisoners, and were restrained only by the speed of their supply train. Ludendorff wondered if he should take Saint Petersburg or Moscow. He was a free agent.

Soon Kerensky and his ministers held just the Winter Palace, a few square yards of space. They were isolated and irrelevant. Nearly all the male soldiers were dead or gone, and Kerensky had just 137 female soldiers, the remnants of the Battalion of Death, who fought against savage odds. Eventually they were overrun, raped, and killed. Kerensky managed to get out of the palace and then out of Moscow. Finally he escaped to America, where he taught in a college. For the rest of his life he would claim to his students that Lenin was an agent of Ludendorff, put in power by German gold. But did anyone care? Meanwhile, Lenin took power and took Russia out of the war.

Ludendorff had done the impossible. No European general, not even Napoleon, had closed down a Russian front. No invader had ever destroyed a Russian government. His success was timeless. In one stroke he had changed the history of the world.

But there was a question lurking behind this victory. Could Ludendorff do something with this success, and swiftly? Could Ludendorff bully Lenin into signing a peace treaty quickly, enabling him to shift his troops to the West and defeat the Allies before the Americans arrived in force?

If he could, then Ludendorff would win his war and become the most successful general of modern times. If not, then Ludendorff would lose the First World War.

CHAPTER 7
Ludendorff Fights Lenin

L UDENDORFF AND LENIN were alike in 1918, even though one was a reactionary and the other a revolutionary. Both had careers that had taken them to dizzying heights. And both saw themselves on the verge of the greatest success that anyone could imagine. Rarely have men of such humble backgrounds risen to such dizzying prospects.

Lenin was the leader of the first Communist state, whose example he believed would inspire workers to overthrow their rickety governments and join his revolution. He had ambitions to send the Red Army to Warsaw and then Berlin. Thence he would send his army to Persia, the Middle East, and—as Ludendorff had dreamed—India, seizing the prize colony of the British Crown. Lenin sensed his revolutions would win these battles. He saw himself sweeping the world. Indeed, in 1920 Lenin would send the Soviet Army to Warsaw to begin this glorious conquest. As historian Richard Pipes of Harvard has noted, Lenin wanted to take Poland and use that as a springboard to take Europe. But amazingly, Lenin's troops were shattered early on by a brave Polish force outside Warsaw in what was called the Miracle on the Vistula, an encounter that decimated the Russians and sent them scurrying back to Moscow in disgrace.

Ludendorff had similar dreams, no less lofty. He dreamed he was leading the great German Army in the decisive battle of the greatest war in history. Soon, he imagined, he would win a Battle of Annihilation, which would make Germany the leading power in the world. As commander of this force, Ludendorff saw himself as the most successful general of the last many centuries, surpassing Napoleon.

Both Lenin and Ludendorff also shared a sense of urgency because their time was running out. Ludendorff had to make a swift peace with Lenin and then move his troops west to fight the Allies because the Americans were on their way. German resources were dwindling and enemy ranks were growing. Every American soldier who arrived in Europe reduced Ludendorff's military advantage, which could collapse any day.

Simultaneously, Lenin was at a pivotal moment. After his Red Guards overthrew Russia's pro-war provisional government in the October Revolution of 1917, Lenin's newly established government decided to withdraw Russia from the world war. His propaganda to get the Russian soldiers to desert and go home had worked well—indeed too well. The Russian soldiers had believed his call for land and freedom, and they were going home to claim them. Soon he would have no army. How, then, could he pacify and control his countryside?

So both men heard a clock ticking. It was in the midst of this that the Central Powers—Germany, Austria-Hungary, Bulgaria, and Turkey—and the new Bolshevik government of Russia met to finalize a treaty that would end the war between them. On December 22, 1917, representatives of these powers convened at a burned-out shell of a town called Brest-Litovsk, located at a rail junction in what is now Belarus. It was a ruined and blackened place, dominated by a ravaged castle that peasants whispered was haunted. Here, from December 22, 1917, through May 15, 1918, the Germans and Russians would parry and duel for the lives and souls of their nations. Ludendorff was there in person, desperately arranging his papers, conferring with delegates, jockeying for power. Lenin would be absent forever but represented by the wily Trotsky, known by some as "the smartest Jew since Moses."

The conference began unsteadily—indeed, for a peace conference, it was a most warlike meeting. Some observers called it a peace of violence. Others called it a peace to end all peace. Sir John Wheeler-Bennett, a brilliant professor at Oxford who spent his life studying German diplomacy, called it "the forgotten peace," a summit so convoluted that most educated people know naught about it except that it was a rabid encounter between Germans and Russians.

But there is no confusion what both sides did behind the scenes. Lenin was trying to destroy Ludendorff's army. Using the money given him by Ludendorff, he was printing every day upward of 500,000 copies of a trail-blazing newspaper, *The Torch*, in German, Hungarian, Romanian, Polish, Yiddish, Turkish, Croatian, Czech, and Bulgarian. That crafty American revolutionary from Harvard, Jack Reed, did most of the writing. Helping him was a mysterious Socialist from Buffalo, New York, named Boris Reinstein, now running Lenin's Bureau of Revolutionary International Propaganda. Also helping him was yet another revolutionary, Albert Rhys Williams, an American friend of Lenin who was a seasoned journalist and a lifelong endorser of Russian Communism. The dynamic revolutionary from Austria, Karl Radek, now head of Lenin's press bureau, put together the ideology. And with them the best presses in Russia were now turning out endless copies, millions a month, all written "for free distribution to our German brothers."

Reed was a staunch Communist, full of hope. He was a stalwart soldier in the Revolution, creating propaganda to convince Germans to cease fighting and to build a workers' state. A mere year later he would see terrible and abominable things in Lenin's Communism. On a train going to Baku for the party, he saw a mass of cadres receiving dozens of bewildered teenage girls, naked under sexy fur coats, accompanied by their pimps, coming aboard the trains to service the Communist delegates. It was shameless rape, of girls only a little beyond puberty, and Reed could barely believe his eyes. Swiftly he would come to view Communism as just another brutal and failed system, one that he had misunderstood and misrepresented to the world. It would break his heart, and this poor dreamer would soon die in a second-rate Moscow hospital, his kidneys broken down, with his last breath repeating four words again and again: "Caught in a trap."

But now he still believed in the struggle, in the leaders, and in the goals. To advance these goals, Reed and Radek orchestrated a stunning campaign. They used a special train and then a fleet of automobiles to distribute their newspapers to special towns along the front, and especially to the German soldiers at the Brest headquarters. These papers were confiscated by German guards, as Reed and Radek expected. But as Reed wrote in the journal *The Liberator* in its edition of January 1919: "At night the real work of distribution began. In isolated spots there were continually secret meetings at which the bundles of propaganda literature were put into the hands of German soldiers. At other points Russian soldiers buried bundles of paper, in places agreed upon, where they were dug up by the Germans."

Reed saw to it that the propaganda was understandable to even the least educated soldier. Under photos of a worker tearing the imperial eagles down from the roof of a palace, Reed wrote explanations:

- "It is easy to overthrow autocracy. Autocracy rests on nothing but the blind obedience of the soldiers."

- "The Russian soldiers merely opened their eyes, and autocracy disappeared."

- "Those who build the palaces should live in them!"

- "For the first time you can see workmen, whose sweat built the palace, enjoying the palace as their home!"

Reed and Radek sent propagandists who spoke German into enemy lines, to meet malcontent soldiers and give talks late in the night. The agitators brought detailed information about their revolution, copies of Soviet decrees, and proclamations to defend workers' rights and families. On several occasions they convinced weary German soldiers of the rightness of their cause. On one glorious occasion, while negotiations were still going on at Brest, the frustrated German authorities had to destroy one of their own camps with artillery, so sympathetic was this camp to Lenin. Yet German repression did no good. As Reed put it, "the poison spread."

The effect of Lenin's work on the German soldiers was decisive. "The influence of Bolshevik propaganda on the masses [of soldiers] was enormous," said one American military observer. "The [German] troops actually melted away before my eyes."

The damage would be massive. Major General Max Hoffmann, the brilliant chief of staff to the German commander in chief on the Russian Front, told it plain to a reporter for the *Chicago Daily News*, which later published his statement on March 13, 1919. Said Hoffman: "Immediately after conquering the Bolsheviks, we were conquered by them. Our victorious army on the Eastern Front became rotten with Bolshevism."

But this success did not advance Lenin's cause. The world revolution of his dreams was not taking place. Yes, the war had mauled the working class of so many nations. Yes, workers should want to lynch the gentlemen who had sent so many to die. But the workers did not want to lynch anyone; they only wanted to go home. A few thousand French soldiers had sat down and had a few strikes, especially at the Paris rail station, the Gare Saint-Lazare. They refused to advance but they were still loyal. They never deserted, even divisions that had lost 80 percent of their men. And the best English soldiers, no matter how battered, were only grumbling. The disaffection was limited. Would the French and British *ever* desert? Lenin was amazed at what he viewed as their lack of class consciousness. These men loved their fellow soldiers and their governments and would never revolt, however dissatisfied they might be after years of war.

Meanwhile, at the conference in Brest, Ludendorff wanted Germany to claim a vast amount of Russian land and money to justify the pain that Germany had endured these war years. He and his delegates demanded huge domains of Georgia, Ukraine, Poland, and Russia's Baltic lands. They wanted more than 1,000,000 square miles of territory, home to 50,000,000 people, all to be added to the German state.

The spoils were staggering. Ludendorff and his men intended to take 33 percent of Russia's rails, 73 percent of Russia's iron, 89 percent of Russia's coal, and 5,000 Russian factories, plus a crushing indemnity of 6,000,000,000 German marks.

To display German power and to awe the delegates, Ludendorff brought his finest soldier, the celebrated pilot Manfred von Richthofen, famously known as the Red Baron, whom Ludendorff paraded around the conference like a prize stallion. He wanted to show off this splendid fighter who had downed eighty Allied pilots. He even had the Red Baron attend the plenary sessions to intimidate the Russians. But did anyone notice that the handsome hero was extraordinarily grim? The brutality of this war was weighing on him. "Death is breathing down my neck," he sighed. "One day it will catch up with me."

Richthofen knew the enemy planes were better now, with supercompression engines that provided greater power. They flew higher and faster and longer and could turn on the proverbial dime. The Red Baron had visited the German assembly plants and knew he and his pilots had no similar improvements on the way. And the Allied pilots were getting better. A New Zealand pilot named Keith Park was invincible. A skilled fighter who would manage the air defense of London for Churchill in the next war, Park was a formidable foe.

To defeat increased numbers of pilots in supercompression planes, which were also arriving in greater numbers, was impossible. To his credit, Richthofen was staying at the front and was still engaged in the fighting. He refused the offer of a cushy job in Berlin and said he would stay with his fellows to the end. But the end was near. Every day he and his friends went up to fight in fewer numbers, and he had no illusions about what would happen in the long term. This war was not a rejuvenation of the fatherland, as Ludendorff's propaganda mills would have it. Instead the war was endless suffering. And Richthofen was not proud of himself for killing so many, even if others were. He could not understand why people thought him wonderful for killing eighty strangers.

Ludendorff, however, was proud of his record. He insisted that it showed how German soldiers could do miracles. Ludendorff also insisted that because of such miracles, the German diplomats at Brest should win stupendous concessions from the war-weary Russians to reward heroic Germans for their sacrifices. Ludendorff's state of mind was obvious when he said at the conference, "If Germany makes peace without profit, Germany has lost the war."

This greed fueled itself, excited the German delegates, and pro-longed the talks. Day and night they produced an endless list of demands that led nowhere.

A strange mechanism was coming into play. As Professor Isabel V. Hull of Cornell University has noted, Ludendorff was not in total charge of events, but he fit the mind-set of the elites. He mir-rored them and they reflected him. And together they made de-mands for the future that grew in a ferocious interplay. Because of this, Ludendorff, Hindenburg, and the other top German officials could never agree on the final list of prizes they wanted. Every week the elites wanted more—indeed more than Germany could absorb.

How had Germany come to this? Greed played a role, but so did the Germans' wanting to be strong *everywhere*. Back in 1915 the senior member of The Duo, Hindenburg, had showed no in-terest in expanding the German Empire. He only wanted to win the war and go home. But now Hindenburg was won over by the dominant Ludendorff, and he too endorsed these expanding claims.

The Kaiser might have saved Germany had he sacked the two and offered the world a reasonable peace. Frederick the Great, when he was at war in 1763 with too many neighbors and was being repeatedly invaded, understood that his nation was on the point of collapse, and he then made several peace treaties. First he made one with Russia and Sweden, then France. He did this by offering peace with no annexations and no indemnities. And this saved his nation from destruction. He himself put it best: "We ought now to think of preserving . . . by way of negotiations, whatever pieces of my territory we can save from the avidity of my enemies."

But the Kaiser wanted glory and was becoming intoxicated with the gains that he imagined he might achieve at the conference. Slowly he began to imagine that if Ludendorff could get staggering concessions in the East and could then free up enough troops to send west, and if his expanded armies could then obtain a speedy victory against the Allies, Germany might become the principal power of the world. On more than one occasion he talked of riding his white stallion down the avenues of Paris in a victory parade at war's end.

So in the battered rail station at Brest, if Ludendorff had made a reasonable long-term strategy, he could have had his finest hour. But instead, sensing how weak the Russians were, Ludendorff forgot how weak he was, and he became more greedy. Worse, his greed was contagious. His allies—the Austrian, Hungarian, Bulgarian, and Turkish delegates—were soon drunk with power too, even though these groups were bled white from the war and should have dreamed only of peace, not annexations. But now the aristocrats

of the Central Powers began to assert some amazing dynastic requirements in addition to the awesome demands of Ludendorff and
Hindenburg, and finally they demanded sixteen huge territories.

The list makes the mind reel:

Wilhelm Karl, the German duke of Enrich, wanted to be king
of Lithuania and was the first to win such a prize. Alas, he was to
reign only from October 9, 1918, to December 14, 1918, some
sixty-seven days. There was no support for his little monarchy and
he was sent packing.

Prince Friedrich Karl of Hessen, from the same dynasty that
produced the idiotic Hessians who fought against the United States
in the American Revolution, wanted the throne of Finland. There
was no throne of Finland, but that did not stop him.

The Kaiser wanted to be the duke of Courland, an ancient land
that he would tear from Lithuania. He also wanted to rule Estonia
and Livonia. And he wanted Poland to be in the hands of a German
prince, who would pretend to rule it as an autonomous state.

Emperor Charles I of Austria wanted one of his men to be king
of Ukraine. King William of Württemberg wanted the Sigmaringen
District, perhaps because of its wonderful castle, which was the
sole jewel in that tarnished crown. The people in Dresden wanted
upper Alsace.

Ludendorff wanted the area in the Crimea where Germans had
settled to be a German province, and he wanted those Germans to be
protected by a German prince, who would pretend that the new nation was autonomous, but who would deliver this land to Germany.

All the Central Powers wanted the oil fields of Baku, the richest
in Europe. The Rockefellers wanted these rich fields, too, but that
is another story.

In a moment of weakness Ludendorff let slip that he needed these territories to maneuver his armies "in the next war." But what war was that? Sometimes Ludendorff said that he expected an eventual war with Austria-Hungary, his current ally. And sometimes he expressed his plan to put the Vatican and all the churches under his control. Sometimes he suggested that he wanted to close the churches and get people to return to the old German gods, like Thor and Frigg. Sometimes he seemed to suggest that he foresaw a union of all German-speaking people under his leadership, with the churches subservient. But his dreams changed every few days, and no man knew what he wanted in the long term. Probably he did not know either.

The situation in Romania was unstable, as it was in Ukraine, so the Germans felt that they should extend their protection there too. Lenin, realizing how much his nation was being threatened, encouraged resistance everywhere. Professor John W. Wheeler-Bennett noted the multiple intrigues and traps that Lenin would use to reinforce his power structure. Ludendorff would soon have to send expeditions to counter Lenin's moves. Lenin's schemes caused problems. Wheeler-Bennett put it plain: "Ludendorff dispatched an expeditionary force to Finland to crush a Bolshevik uprising; another expedition penetrated to Baku; a third occupied the Crimean ports. An army of occupation was maintained in Romania. Grand ducal governments were in the process of creation in Courland, Lithuania, Livonia and Estonia. And the German colonies in the Crimea were urged to appeal to the Kaiser for annexation."

These expeditions would require the hugest effort. In Finland a civil war broke out on January 27, 1918, only days after the Brest conference began. Ludendorff had to send some 13,000 crack

troops to his White Army allies in the north to enforce his preroga-
tives. The Soviets, meanwhile, sent troops to their Red Army allies
in the south. Then, to quote Milton, "all Hell broke loose."

In the battle of Helsinki on April 18, 1918, only weeks after
the treaty was signed at Brest on March 3, 1918, the Germans captured 8,000 Red Army soldiers. That same month, a German naval
squadron was sent to bombard the Finnish coast. Though these
events may sound like successes for Ludendorff, they were defeats
because they required time and men that Ludendorff could not af-
ford. He needed victory in the West, and he needed it now. Had he
and his colleagues been less greedy, and had they obtained a peace
that was less difficult to maintain, their situation might have been
easier.

As it was, it was impossible. Soon the Germans had to go to
Baku, to keep the great oil wells secure. Then the Germans needed
to hold the ports of the Crimea. Then more troops would have
to hold German privileges in Romania. To hold onto the various
German pretenses in the great city of Kiev, they needed three entire
divisions.

The time had come for Germans to scale back their wishes.
But the Kaiser and Ludendorff would have none of this. Indeed,
the greed of the German elites increased. Soon the Kaiser let slip
his dream to carve up the British, French, and Belgian holdings in
Africa and add *them* to his crown. They now bandied about the term
German Middle Africa. They wanted a belt of German land from
eastern to western Africa, straight across the continent, to show the
power of their arms. No Germans explained what value there was
in African colonies. Most cost more to run than they brought in
revenue. And the center of Africa was especially worthless. These

Erich Ludendorff and Adolf Hitler

Young Erich Ludendorff, circa 1892

His first wife, Margarethe,
in 1915, before her two sons died

Franz Pernet, son of Ludendorff's
first wife, killed in his offensives

Erich Pernet, stepson also killed
in Ludendorff's offensives

His first wife, Margarethe,
in mourning for her sons

His second wife, Mathilde von Kemnitz—note swastikas embroidered on dress

The "stab-in-the-back" cartoon, 1919—
Germans blaming Jews for the loss of World War I

Ludendorff late in life

His grave in Bavaria makes no specific
military reference; there is just a sword

lands held a few products but they could be extracted only with herculean effort. Still, the Kaiser and Ludendorff wanted these lands. They wished to be *seen* as powerful. They wanted the prestige. So they sought dominion over Europe and Central Africa, imagining an empire that would stagger the world.

Once as a young man the Kaiser had written a plaintive letter to his relative Queen Victoria, begging her to give him a particular mountain in Africa simply because he did not own any mountains there. It was weird and illogical. Several other monarchs were similar. The half-mad King Leopold II of Belgium wanted, and seized, all of Congo, a land larger than Texas, and had it registered as his personal property. Caesar, when he wanted to add Egypt to the Roman Empire, had similar delusions. Alexander the Great, when he allegedly burst into tears because he had no more lands to conquer, was another such zealot. To write a cogent history of such men, whether they be named Ludendorff or Leopold, is a challenge. They wanted much their nations did not need.

And things got worse. Before long, schemers in Berlin were talking of transforming the Crimea into a German Riviera. Some had visions of obtaining a swathe of land from there to Persia to Afghanistan, and from there to India—the gilded mirage of India that kept coming up on their horizons.

Of course Germans often claimed they were merely protecting the interests of Germans who were there. Humorist Will Rogers, the man with the best wisecracks in America, quipped that building protectorates sounded like the idea of China sending gunboats up the Mississippi to protect the Chinese laundries in towns on the riverbank. They would not be there to help the laundries. They would be there to help themselves.

While all these schemers were plotting the future of the world after the war, the war was not over. On the western front, the Germans were still fighting the British Empire, the French Empire, and the Belgians. And soon an unknown number of Americans were due to arrive.

The top German writer on Americans was a wild-eyed novelist named Karl May, who composed weird Western novels with an Aryan character named Shatterhand, who always defeated the Yanks even when outnumbered ten to one. Millions of his books were sold in Germany. Even the young Hitler read them. Amazingly, May had never visited America. Still, his books—which showed that one German was equal to ten Americans—were cherished, for they told Germans what they wanted to hear. Though they were trash, the books convinced so many that in any conflict, Germans would destroy Americans in all circumstances.

Ludendorff's staff, in a euphoria of confidence, worked to convince him that with a swift transfer of troops, the German forces would have a numerical advantage. But the 1,000,000 German troops tied down in Russia were mostly required there. Lenin had sensed this from the beginning. "As a result of this robber peace," Lenin once told his cabinet, "Germany will have to maintain larger, not fewer, forces in the East." And to make matters worse, the German forces there were on the brink of exhaustion. Every soldier on the eastern front wanted to go home. And each soldier soon heard disturbing rumors that he would have to go directly to the western front instead, to fight a last battle. Soldiers there, the rank and file, had done too many miracles, and they were uninterested in these dreams of glory. When reporters asked what they thought of these plans, these horrors without end, these triumphs without victory, the soldiers would ask why they should die for places they could not find on the map.

If Ludendorff had understood how exhausted and disenchanted his troops were, he might have made a simple peace with Russia, then moved his 1,000,000-man army swiftly to the West and sought only a partial victory there. He could have fought a final battle, *not* the fabled Battle of Annihilation. He could have waged a defensive battle and then called for a "peace of the brave," a magnanimous peace hurting no man. It might have included border adjustments but nothing serious. There would be no land stolen from Poland or Belgium, Russia or France, no demand for gold or indemnities. Such a peace could have lasted and there would have been no chance of a new world war.

If he were not so overworked, perhaps Ludendorff might have considered this. But Ludendorff was driven. This last year of the war, Ludendorff's staff sensed that he was going to collapse, and they came together in hushed meetings. Some thought they heard him sobbing. When he quivered and started to shake, they thought he might fall and never rise again. What concerned them here was that Ludendorff dominated Hindenburg, and the two dominated the government. If Ludendorff collapsed, the nation might collapse with him.

They summoned a psychiatrist, Dr. Hochheimer, to analyze the situation. He said that the problem was that the general's life was all worry and strain. Nothing involved joy and laughter. As the doctor put it: "The man is utterly lonely."

Hochheimer said that Ludendorff had to slow down, stop rushing his food, start breathing deeply, sing some songs, walk in the woods, and listen to the splashing of the brook. Ludendorff should read poems and look at flowers.

For a time Ludendorff did as he was told. He ate slowly, took time off, and even sang some folk songs. Things looked better, and Hochheimer helped Ludendorff avert a breakdown.

But Ludendorff, after recovering, returned to his old ways and started to make a new and dangerous plan. He planned to fight the last battle, the fabled Battle of Annihilation, to win the war with one stupendous victory. Unaware that his men were dying on their feet, Ludendorff pressed for a stunning success, one that would be the biggest of the war.

But things had gotten worse, not better. The British were discovering the power of tanks and were improving them, making them faster and stronger. They had learned how to use them effectively. Tanks were no longer employed to support the infantry but were now understood as an independent force. British officers were sending them forward in packs, ahead of the infantry, cutting gaping holes in the German lines, sowing panic in their wake.

The situation was doubly problematic in the German Air Force. The average pilot got up each morning expecting to die. Ludendorff's eldest stepson admitted this in a letter home. The pilots posted to an average German squadron had five weeks to live. They were like the poor German submarine crews who now averaged four missions at sea and then died.

Incredibly, at this juncture in 1918, Lenin and Ludendorff both thought they could send an army to take India. The idea was lunacy. But both wanted India now.

Ludendorff decided that he needed extra power to carry out these schemes, so he challenged the authority of the Kaiser. He waited for his moment. When the Kaiser accepted a lower-ranking general's opinion on a matter concerning Poland, Ludendorff exploded that the Kaiser did not have the right to go around him and stormed out of the room, slamming the door like a spoiled child. Ludendorff followed up with a memo protesting that the Kaiser did not have confidence in him and sent his resignation. The Kaiser, frightened at the idea of waging a war without his heroes, capitulated. Not until the last days of the war would the Kaiser have the courage to challenge these men.

At Brest the Germans did all they could to get Lenin to accept their terms. Their dream was to release the 1,000,000 German troops tied down in Russia and move them west to make the breakthrough. This dream had problems, however. The Germans, for this most important battle of their lives, did not have an objective. Whenever Ludendorff was asked about his objective, he would answer that he would make a hole in the enemy line and the rest would take care of itself. That was his answer every time he was asked.

But if Germany knocked the Allies back and inflicted, say, 100,000 casualties, and then if the United States brought in 100,000 replacements the next month, as they were now doing every month, what then? What victory could Germany have when it could not replace its casualties, while the Allies could?

Worse, if Ludendorff's troops could not pierce the line, what backup plan did he have? Ludendorff did not account for failure—his offensive had to work. But would it? This situation in 1918 was like Germany's situation in 1914. Both times the German generals had a risky plan that *had* to work because they could see no alternative if it failed.

But the plan of 1918 could not work, for it was as insubstantial as the plan of 1914. To break through, according to Jean de

Bloch, Ludendorff needed an eight-to-one ratio of his troops to enemy troops. Ludendorff's troops, even with all the reinforcements from Russia, would outnumber the Allies three to one at best. And this supposed that Ludendorff could get all those troops from the East immediately. Yet every day Ludendorff received demands for more troops to pacify his new empire. They had to be sent to Poland, Finland, Romania, Ukraine, Lithuania, Livonia, Estonia, Baku, Odessa, and other annexed places on the map, to enforce Germany's imagined rights. Ludendorff's peace was so severe and caused so many problems that instead of releasing troops, it asked for more.

Lenin, armed with his millions in German gold and with the power of his newly acquired state, was shaking Ludendorff's ramshackle empire to the core. He was sending agitators to corrupt the German troops in Russia. And those troops, bone weary, were listening to his siren song, which was saying, in effect: *We offer you peace, land, and freedom. Lay down your arms. Do not be the last man to die for a mistake. Go home to people who love you.*

No matter how Ludendorff tried, he could not disengage enough forces from the East. A peace like Brest has to be enforced. And those German soldiers, whom he wanted to detach and send west, would bring problems of their own. Often they were corrupting loyal German troops. Said one German officer: "We got to the point where we did not dare transfer certain of our eastern divisions to the West."

Despite such reservations, some soldiers were shipped west because they were badly needed there. These men became rowdy, fired their rifles from the trains, and they even threw grenades. Some soldiers went onto the roofs of the cars and cut wires in the stations. Sometimes they disconnected the cars or put sand in the engines. Other soldiers fled into the woods, where they lived for weeks by hunting game, which they said was more honorable than hunting men. The authorities kept these outbursts hushed, but civilians heard what was happening and could see the subversive words written on many railway cars: *Cattle to be slaughtered for the Kaiser* and *Dead meat for the German Army*. In one poignant case the words read: *Why are you doing this to us?* Another message said, *We are your children!*

Clearly the propaganda of Jack Reed and Karl Radek was doing its work. It was so effective that when German soldiers from the Russian Front returned to Austria and Germany, the most extreme were confined to political quarantine camps, where officers tried to reeducate them with promises, patriotic literature, and good food. But this was usually too little, too late. The men only wanted to go home.

The full impact of the Reed/Radek propaganda has never been fully analyzed. One part of the problem is that Radek was murdered by Stalin, and he became a nonperson in the land of the Soviets. One could not study him or praise him. Reed, meanwhile, became basically anti-Communist and died in a second-class Moscow hospital. Only his lover from Oregon, Louise Bryant, was with him when he perished, and in the USSR his reputation declined instantly. Clearly the Soviets eliminated both Reed and Radek, early on, one by neglect, the other by murder. As a result, no man in the USSR would dare tell the tale of how well these two dreamers assaulted the German Army and made it a less effective fighting force. And it was all forgotten.

But truth to tell, the work of Reed and Radek made it impossible for Ludendorff to extract all the troops he wanted from

Russia, in the state of mind that he wanted them. The adventure was summed up by Reed in the title of one of his fiery articles: "How Soviet Russia Conquered Imperial Germany." Proudly Reed told how they indoctrinated whole German companies into a posture of pure pacifism.

And the pacifism grew. Soon antiwar networks were growing, to hide deserters and to spirit them away. Pacifist groups were formed to give boys papers, passports, ration cards, maps, and guides to get them to the Netherlands. The papers were done so well that the boys passed every checkpoint.

The Dutch met these deserters warmly. If an asylum-seeker stumbled onto a Dutch highway and met a squad of policemen, the officers would give the young man a friendly handshake. "Be glad that you are here," they would say. "We Dutch wish for peace, and you are welcome here."

Ludendorff was enraged that the Netherlands gave these men asylum, but asylum was their tradition. During the Reformation they gave asylum to thousands of Englishmen. They gave Descartes asylum. And now they were giving asylum to 20,000 peace-seekers from Germany, with the number growing every day.

Not all German troops were deserting. Some would fight. But even these were stunned that they were being ordered to the West without a visit home. And almost none was enthusiastic. The days when they put flowers on their rifles and sang marching songs were over.

Instead one might hear someone whispering a now-familiar refrain about how Germany should accept even a severe peace from the Allies. A powerful slogan spread, a widely quoted phrase used by a Social Democrat named August Bebel to caution the German military in 1911: "Better an end with horrors, than horrors without end."

And horrors were increasing. News came that the new American Army might arrive soon. Sensing that time was on their side, the Russian delegates at Brest were hostile to conceding any territories to the Central Powers. Count Otto von Czernin, the leader of the Austrian delegation, returned this contempt when talking to Communist delegate Adolph Joffe, saying that peace would not be possible if the Russians insisted on everyone's having the right of self-determination. If the Russians insisted on that, the delegates might as well go home.

But he was bluffing. Warlike words from Czernin did not frighten Joffe, who responded confidently: "I very much hope that we shall be able to raise the flag of revolution in your own country."

A famous Siberian delegate named Anastasia Bizenko talked matter-of-factly to Prince Leopold of Bavaria, telling him how she had killed a Russian governor in 1905. She had put her pistol under a petition, and when she handed the paper to him, she blew his guts out. This got her a life sentence in a Siberian jail, but Communists broke open the prison and freed her. She was the star of the Russian delegation, this quiet grey-haired assassin. And at Brest-Litovsk, she was sizing up the weakening elites of Germany. She handled her champagne well, she played Schubert into the night, and she showed that she was as sophisticated as they were. But deep down she would have been glad to kill them.

Then there was the grey-bearded peasant named Roman Stashkov. How he became a delegate is a tale worth sharing: On their way to the conference, the Russians realized they did not have a peasant to represent that class while they negotiated with the lords

of the enemy forces. This would not do. A proletarian movement
without a proletarian was like a carriage without a horse. Clearly
they needed a commoner. So they looked for one.

On the highway they espied an old Russian in a peasant coat with
a knapsack, trudging along. He had a great grey beard and a brick-
tanned face and looked as if he had seen many things in his time.

"Are you a revolutionary?" they asked him.

"Yes," he answered, sensing that this was the answer they
wanted. "I'm going to Moscow," he added defensively.

"Then delay and come with us," they told him. "Come and negotiate with the Germans for your country's independence."

The peasant was not inclined, and he made matters awkward by
addressing one Russian delegate as "Master."

"You'll have plenty to drink," they pleaded.

This changed his mind, and he came cheerfully.

At the negotiations he said nothing. It was only when he was
brought to the state dinner that the old man charmed the elegant
German butler by the honest way he talked.

"Do you want white wine or red?" the butler asked him.

"Which is stronger?" Stashkov inquired.

"Here, the red," the butler responded.

"Then the red, if you please," he answered.

So he got cheerfully drunk. To him, the wine was more interesting than Ludendorff's boundaries or indemnities. He shoveled
vast amounts of food and wine into his bearded face, thanked the
German butlers with profusion, and showed confusion only over
the multiple forks at his place. But finally he decided they were all
good for picking the food between his teeth. He smiled and told the

aristocratic delegates that he had never had so much free wine or so many good times.

The aristocrats from the Central Powers found him vastly more pleasant than they found the other Communist delegates, who were out for blood, not wine. They saw him as more agreeable than the irascible Leon Trotsky, the top Marxist revolutionary, who was dreaming up ways to antagonize them.

Beyond Russia, momentous things were happening. Every fragment of news indicated that on the western front, the British and French were given a new lease on life just knowing the Yanks were coming. When a French boy got his draft papers this last year of the war, he saw American and French flags intertwined at the top of the summons, and every French officer would promise: "We shall ask no offensives of you until the Americans have come."

Germany's days were numbered. It might win a victory or two, but like the Greek king Pyrrhus, who won Pyrrhic victories against Rome in ancient times, the triumphs would come at such cost that they were tantamount to defeats. The Russians saw that Ludendorff was similar to Pyrrhus, a successful fighter but a man on the point of collapse. In such a case they would not need to negotiate. All they had to do was stall until Ludendorff's army died.

So stall they did. Truth to tell, the Russian revolutionaries obtained great joy in antagonizing these lords who had murdered their brothers. And no man among the Russians loved baiting the aristocrats more than Trotsky, the Russian commissar of foreign affairs, who taunted them with glee. He felt that the German elites could not possibly order their troops to renew the war in the East, so he did not have to respect them as a military force.

This was dangerous because Trotsky was the one who did not have a reliable army. Indeed, he had no army at all. He had examined the Russian trenches behind the conference and was shocked to find them empty. He tried to convince himself that the Germans in like manner had no army that they could use. He imagined that the German soldiers would desert if Ludendorff ordered them back to the war.

This was a colossal error. Trotsky misjudged Ludendorff's power and influence, the power that had made him the dictator of Germany, far above the Kaiser. Nor did Trotsky understand that Ludendorff was committed to winning his *entire* list of demands against Russia.

So when Trotsky received the terms offered by the Germans, he dared reject them with all the loftiness of an emperor. "The terms proposed to us by the governments of Germany and Austria-Hungary are in fundamental conflict with the interests of all peoples," he declared imperiously, to a thunderstruck delegation. He said there was no way Russia would accept them. So on February 10, 1918, he declared his famous response, "No war, no peace!" and stormed out. He was convinced that the Germans could not ask their troops to fight again.

The Germans were shocked. Ludendorff's trusted military strategist, Max Hoffmann, said with amazement, "Unheard-of." No defeated power had ever stormed out of a peace conference.

As Trotsky left, Hoffmann inquired how the Germans should keep in touch with the Russians, but Trotsky did not answer. He was certain that the German troops would refuse to fight, the conference would dissolve, the delegates would go home, and the war would end.

But on February 17, 1918, Ludendorff called Lenin's bluff and sent his weary legions east once more, into Ukraine, Belarus, and the Baltic nations. Riga, the capital of Latvia, fell in days, and the German troops continued the penetration.

Lenin realized that without a peace treaty, his new Communist state would die. A peace accord, even a "robber peace" as he termed it, would allow his young Communist government time to consolidate power in Russia. So he insisted that his cabinet sign whatever the Germans offered. It was either that or the death of the first Communist state.

Craftily the Germans upped the ante. After a nerve-wracking delay of four days, the Germans began negotiations again but demanded great new escalations—whopping unexpected concessions in Latvia, Estonia, Ukraine, and Finland—all within a two-day deadline.

Lenin scanned the terms, then told his aghast ministers that they would sign. If they refused, he would resign and his government would fall. He thundered and stormed and shouted and satirized. And in several ways, it was his finest moment.

It took hours to convince them. But he explained it again and again. This robber peace would require huge forces to implement it. And even then, those German forces would encounter major passive resistance. The agreement, Lenin knew, could not be carried out. It was not as awful as it appeared. And for these reasons, he insisted, the Russians would sign.

Eventually he battered his ministers into submission. His cabinet signed the document. A few abstained but no one voted against it. Trotsky vanished for days, devastated over the new losses because they were entirely his fault.

So on March 3, 1918, Ludendorff got his treaty, for which he and his kind had sacrificed the best boys of a generation. But what would it give? The conquered lands surrendered their wealth slowly. Ludendorff obtained some trainloads of grain, but to get more, he had to assign thousands of troops to control these new territories.

Meanwhile the passive resistance became huge. In Odessa, an airplane factory was set on fire. Ammunition dumps blew up unexpectedly. Partisans murdered isolated bands of German soldiers. Peasant risings erupted.

Slowly, some German troops were released for the West, a few thousand weary and disgruntled men who had done too much, gone too far, and served too long. They had been promised leave to go back home. When they were sent directly to the western front, they felt betrayed, and many went home anyway.

People in the Allied nations were aghast when they saw the severity of the terms Ludendorff had inflicted upon a battered Russia. From that point onward, the western statesmen ceased any talk about a compromise peace. Wrote Oxford historian John W. Wheeler-Bennett: "The peace of Brest-Litovsk . . . showed clearly to the world what mercy the conquered enemies of Germany might expect [if they lost the war]. The effect in the Allied countries was a grim tightening of the belts and an increased determination to destroy the regime which could make such a peace." World leaders now saw Ludendorff as a megalomaniac, and they regarded his Germany as what Romans used to call an "enemy of the human race."

They may have been correct. Germany was indeed becoming an enemy of the world. It was a country that enslaved its neighbors and its own people at the same time. It sent torpedoes into any ships it pleased, spewed poison on the battlefield, and practiced something similar to genocide in both Africa and Europe.

In their colony in German Southwest Africa, or Namibia, the Germans had started practicing their extermination skills with their fabled efficiency even before World War I. When the Herero people protested the way the Germans were confiscating their cattle and land, a governor named Heinrich Göring unleashed the German Army on them. In a three-year campaign of extermination, from 1904 through 1907, Göring drove the warriors and their families into the desert and allegedly poisoned their wells, thus dropping the population from 80,000 to 15,000, in what the surviving Herero call "the first genocide." Göring's son Hermann later became Hitler's right hand and maintained the family traditions. Later still, he was sentenced to die at Nuremberg for killing vast numbers of Jews.

Now, in 1917 and 1918, people were beginning to ask what had happened to Germany. How had one of the most educated nations come to such barbarism? How had the Kaiser, who once had the courage to fire the powerful Bismarck, become helpless before the less imposing Ludendorff? And how did Germany develop such greed? How had Germany, through its elites, its propaganda agencies, its educational system, and its military castes, managed to induce on itself a collective madness that rendered the nation demented?

Far away in Eugene, Oregon, an editor at the *Eugene Register-Guard* penned an editorial that appeared in the March 9, 1918, issue. Titled "When Nations Go Mad," the timely article showed great insight on this unexplored topic.

"Can nations become insane?" the editor wrote. "Every effort of our own to find a rational explanation for the conduct of the German people results in the conclusion that it is an indubitable case of mutual aberration. Their methods of reasoning cannot be reduced to any accepted forms of logic. Their conclusions do not inevitably follow from their premises. . . . They neither think nor act like normal people. It seems incredible that fifty million people can go mad together, but every other theory has proved itself inadequate."

In similar fashion Dr. Gerald D. Feldman, a historian at the University of California–Berkeley, who wrote ten books on Germany, saw in this era "a complete breakdown of substantial reality." Some historians suggest that Germany in the world wars presents a collective insanity that started with Ludendorff in 1914 and ended with the suicide of Hitler, who so resembled him, in 1945.

Ludendorff did not do this alone. It is simply that Ludendorff fit the zeitgeist of his nation so well that he was never resisted. He was endorsed by the elites and by the Kaiser, and practically no one stood against him. In the entire Reichstag, only one German politician spoke out against his peace of plunder, a Social Democrat named Hugo Haase—but this dissident was ignored. When he kept complaining, he was murdered.

The nation understood that it was unwise to challenge Ludendorff's positions at Brest. Besides, all other politicians lined up behind Ludendorff. These politicians felt, like Ludendorff, that since Germans had suffered much, they should receive much, to give meaning to the suffering of the nation.

The Treaty of Brest-Litovsk served to solidify popular American support for the Allied forces. One of America's patriotic musicians,

George M. Cohan, late one night penned a song that should have sent a chill down the spine of any German. It referred to Europe as the land "Over There" and it became the anthem of the American soldiers in training:

> Over there, Over there,
> Send the word, send the word, over there
> That the Yanks are coming, the Yanks are coming,
> The drums rum-tumming everywhere.
> So prepare, say a prayer,
> Send the word, send the word, to beware—
> We'll be over, we're coming over,
> And we won't be back till it's over, over there.

To win the war, Ludendorff would now have to defeat not only Britain, Canada, Australia, South Africa, Rhodesia, New Zealand, India, France, the French Empire, and Belgium but also the full force of the United States, a prime economic power. Germany, an empire with dwindling resources and an army already stretched thin, was now fighting nations whose combined populations totaled 1,000,000,000. It was Ludendorff and Germany against the world. Thanks to his decision not to make peace in 1916 and his ferocious way of negotiating in 1918, the situation was clear: Germany had to win against 1,000,000,000 people or fall.

CHAPTER 8

Ludendorff Attacks in the West to Win Before the Americans Arrive

Now that Ludendorff had his treaty signed, he made plans to move his troops from the eastern front in Russia to the western front in Europe. In the spring of 1918, he planned a series of attacks on the western front that would make the deepest advances since 1914. These attacks were called the Ludendorff Offensives.

The size was unprecedented. Ludendorff planned to hit his enemy with 6,000 pieces of artillery, 3,000 mortars, and new squadrons of storm troopers, his best men, who would cut deep into enemy territory. These men would pass around the better-defended points on the front line and wreak havoc in the rear. They would use the German-invented flamethrower, plus clouds of the best new poison gas. They would send barrages of artillery that would creep forward just ahead of the troops. When exhausted, the troops on the front line would lie low while other German soldiers would leapfrog over them, maintaining the terror, all so quickly that the enemy could not react in time.

The plan was not original—it was an idea copied from the 1916 offensive of General Aleksei Brusilov of Russia—but it was incredibly solid, and it promised spectacular results. There was one difference, however. In 1916, Brusilov did not have to contend with British tanks, which could have stopped him cold. Ludendorff had too quickly discounted this fancy British invention, which the Allies were finally bringing to the field in great numbers. He believed that tanks were slow lumbering beasts that could be destroyed by artillery fire and were therefore worthless. He saw them as a gadget that the world would forget. He did not understand that the newest model of British tanks was smaller, faster, tougher, and more maneuverable. They would surprise him.

Finally, Ludendorff did not accept the information offered by Count Heinrich von Bernstorff, the last German ambassador to the United States, who told anyone who would listen that American men were tough and that American reserves were "inexhaustible." Ludendorff did find the coming of the Americans to be problematic for his propaganda machine, so he ordered a blackout. German soldiers on leave were surprised to find that people back home had no idea that Yanks were fighting on the western front, nor that at least 100,000 of them were arriving every month.

Now, with the German troops released from the East, Ludendorff believed this new offensive would achieve his breakthrough and that such a breakthrough would automatically win the war—two very separate assumptions. If there had been a German politician like Churchill or Roosevelt, he would have asked Ludendorff withering questions, like: Are you trying to destroy the French Army? The British Army? Are you trying to take Paris? Or are you trying to drive the British into the sea?

Ludendorff seemed to be entertaining all of these options at the same time. At any moment one of these options dominated, and at other moments another seemed at the fore. And which was feasible? Was only the last option, driving the smaller British Army into the sea, plausible?

Was there any way to take Paris when it was so well defended? And even if Ludendorff could take it, couldn't the French Army retreat to Bordeaux and wait for more Americans to arrive? Was only the smaller British Army a feasible target?

No civilians in Germany dared ask. The German soldiers were risking their nation's life on the hunch of an old battered man, who in the view of many was irrational and in the view of some was insane.

But one must credit Ludendorff on his audacity. Ludendorff and his men were preparing the greatest advance of the Great War. Their onslaught was meticulous and unprecedented. Especially brilliant was the deployment of the storm troopers. These were units of the best soldiers in the army, who were trained to avoid all strong points, to go forward in small packs, under a creeping artillery barrage. They would go just before the advancing German troops and level any strategic point they wished.

The Germans also brought in a fearsome new weapon: the Paris Gun, a monster piece of artillery of some 256 tons that fired shells seventy-five miles distant, in a great arc twenty-five miles up into the air. It took eighty men to manage this monstrosity—to move it, load it, and fire it. Each shell took three minutes to reach its target. It was difficult to use, cost millions, and was so inaccurate that you could fire it only into a city, like Paris. Even then, no one could predict where the shell would fall. This gun was made to inspire terror. It was a murderous toy that would appeal only to brutal men. Years later, Hitler would build a similar gun for himself. Ludendorff used his on Paris; Hitler used his on Warsaw.

Two or three hundred tanks would have been a better invest-
ment of men and metal, which is the method the British used. The
small new British tanks moved swiftly, sowing a special kind of
terror that was far more effective than Ludendorff's wild and im-
precise monster gun.

One concern pervaded the minds of Ludendorff's staff as they
prepared his offensive. The younger officers examined his plans
and worried that there was no objective beyond a vague hope for
a breakthrough that would bring victory. A shocked Rupprecht,
crown prince of Bavaria, who ably commanded an entire German
army, pointed it out. "There is no great operational goal behind the
attacks," he said.

Ludendorff's first campaign, Operation Michael, did start well.
In this, the most intelligent assault of the Ludendorff Offensives, he
aimed a withering attack at the hinge point where the French and
British armies were joined—inevitably a weak link. Here he may have
been targeting the British, whose army there was feeble. It was full
of conscripts, mostly underage boys, and because the shrewd British
prime minister David Lloyd George wanted to parcel out soldiers in
small quantities so that the overly bold British generals would not
spend their soldiers' lives too freely, this army appeared weak.

Ludendorff's storm troopers hit the British/French hinge on
March 10, 1918. The two Allied armies fell back and separated,
and for a time there was a hole on the western front, a gap of forty
miles that might have allowed the fabled breakthrough.

Some experts, like Wheeler-Bennett of Oxford, believe that if
the German forces here had had the three divisions of their army
that were occupying Kiev, then Ludendorff *might* have won his
campaign at this point. Others, however, have suggested that any

military campaign without an overall objective is doomed, and this was the case with all of Ludendorff's campaigns, from the first year of the war to the last.

Unfortunately for Ludendorff, the British refused to scatter after the breakthrough. They recoiled like a boxer hit hard and then regained their footing and came back. This same British force still blocked the way to the ports and held the vital rail link at Amiens. Somehow this particular British army, understrength and with underage conscripts, transformed itself in an instant and behaved with utterly stupefying courage. The men redeployed and then returned to the field like exterminating angels.

Ludendorff tried to improvise. He launched a second offensive called Operation Georgette on April 11. It came within fifteen miles of the ports. The British general there, Douglas Haig, was alleged to be a fool but was now acting like an experienced warrior. He refused to panic and wrote a stirring communiqué that is remembered to this day: "There is no other course open to us but to fight it out. Every position must be held to the last man. There must be no retirement. With our backs to the wall and believing in the justice of our cause, each of us must fight to the end. The safety of our homes and the Freedom of Mankind alike depend upon the conduct of each one of us at this critical moment."

And then these soldiers returned with a rumble and a roar. The Germans had penetrated and had made a deep salient, a bulge, which was formidable, yes, but which presented some fetching opportunities. The English saw that they could slash the Germans on three sides at once, and they did this, ferociously. The Germans in the salient were slaughtered, and the survivors fell back, bleeding and reeling. They were dying by the thousands.

Thus ended the German idea of pushing the British Army into the sea.

Amid the deaths of so many, the death of one special man, far away, went unnoticed. Gavrilo Princip, the student who had shot the archduke and started this war in 1914, died on April 28, 1918, in a prison cell in Serbia. He had been suffering from so many ills that we can only guess what killed him. He had contracted tuberculosis; he had an infected arm that had been amputated; he had pus-filled blisters covering his body; and he had been miserable in his tiny cell, a place so cold that it killed even the fleas.

He understood that millions were dying in this war he had started, and he knew that his people were drowning in their blood. Indeed, the percentage of war dead in Serbia was the highest of all nations in the war. This might have depressed a normal boy, but Princip felt that he had started the war for the good of his people and that the price being paid was not excessive. He believed that this horrible war would somehow make his people happy. He never conceded that he had caused the worst European war in history up to that time. He never imagined that Serbia would be an unhappier nation, stocked with countless widows and orphans, with ruined roads and bridges, and with battlefields that looked like the far side of the moon.

He felt no guilt. His only regret was that when he killed the archduke, he also killed the man's wife. He did not want any unnecessary dead and was clear on that. It did not occur to him that there were *millions* of unnecessary dead because of him, in his nation and every nation.

The number of German losses in the Ludendorff Offensive soon equaled the losses of the Allied forces, and the slaughter was huge on all sides. The German officers did not mention the word *victory* because it seemed obscene.

Ludendorff now unleashed attacks elsewhere, this time against the French, and again it seemed that he could not see his goal. Was he trying to destroy the French? Outflank them? Take Paris? Or rack up casualties?

The French fought like heroes. They were defending their homes, and they called their force a "sacred union." Even French Communists who distrusted their capitalist government and French royalists who dismissed their republican state fought ferociously. Cartier, the famed jeweler, was so grateful to the tank commanders for saving Paris in these battles that he designed the superb Tank Watch to thank them, a design that is sold proudly to this day. These heroes scattered Ludendorff's attacks, shouting the celebrated phrase from Joan of Arc, "On les aura!"

Ludendorff was dispersing his efforts, as he had been doing for years. Rupprecht, crown prince of Bavaria, understood better than most how severely German soldiers were being scattered, indeed dissipated, and therefore were fighting to no effect. He wrote, "Now we have lost the war."

Ludendorff started Operation Gneisenau on June 9, 1918, but did so badly. A tough, ferocious officer from the French colonial forces named Charles Mangin effected a withering counterattack. General Mangin, called "the Butcher" for the way that he could endure casualties, was subtle and brutal at the same time. Craftily he drove 150 tanks precisely to the points where the Germans would not expect them. And the Germans were slaughtered.

The Germans had no tanks. They had *plans* for tanks, but they were making a mere twenty tanks that year, all of low-grade steel

that shattered when hit. The *Titanic* was made of the same dam-
nable steel, and it shattered when that vessel hit an iceberg, with
results too well-known. Worse, these twenty tanks were slow and
made good targets. All in all, the German tanks were few, slow,
and easy to kill. They were moving coffins and no one took them
seriously.

Meanwhile the Allied tanks caused terror. When they came
upon German soldiers, even the elite storm troopers ran.

Ludendorff's efforts to terrorize civilians with the Paris Gun
had no result. The great gun fired a total of 370 shells, cost millions, and killed only 256 Frenchmen, all civilians. A few German
snipers in the trees could have done more. These pathetic acts of
German terror only provoked the French and mobilized them for a
final victory, which they perceived was coming soon.

When the lean starving soldiers of Germany came to the great
military warehouses of the Allies, they stared at the supplies of their
enemy. They were astonished at the volumes of meat, wine, and
liquor; the bandages, anesthetic, and medicines; the trucks, tires,
and gas; the movie theaters, libraries, and canteens. These were
the supplies that had been scarce for them these lean years. Again
and again the official German records show a breakdown in discipline whenever their troops came upon an Allied warehouse.
Ludendorff's propaganda had assured his men that England was
being starved out and that American supplies could not get to
Europe. He had lied.

German soldiers were enraged. Their government had been lying all these years. How could they now respect officers who had
been telling them that German submarines were starving out the
British?

The soldiers formed mobs, and the mobs plundered the store-houses. Drunken German troopers would be seen, each with his bottle, eating meat, singing songs, and dreaming of home.

A German lieutenant named Rudolf Binding recorded his shock. "I began to see curious sights. Strange figures, which looked little like soldiers, [who] certainly showed no sign of advancing." He looked on amazed as he saw German troops playing around like goofy schoolboys. Some wore top hats, or curtains; some had chickens under their arms, and others drove cows through the streets, meandering unsteadily, passing him drunkenly. He turned into an alley and saw it running with wine and met a German officer who confessed, "I cannot get my men out of this wine cellar without shooting them." Some soldiers said they were happy for the first time in years.

The more conservative German officers were furious at this insubordination. But one kinder officer remarked, "What is so surprising about a starving soldier's gorging himself in a storehouse? What is shocking if this miserable man takes a drink?"

The problems with the wonderful British scotch and beer at the warehouses became chronic. An anonymous wag made a quip that the entire campaign might be lost, "not for lack of German fighting spirit, but on account of the abundance of British drinking spirits."

German advances were real but uncertain. Before, the German Air Force would protect its soldiers and would strafe any advancing enemy soldiers. Indeed the English verb *strafe* came into use during this war, in 1915, derived from a German word that means "to punish"—as in the German phrase "Gott strafe England," or "God punish England." The once-powerful German Air Force had done that early in the war. But that magnificent force was mostly dead.

Symbolically, the Red Baron himself died in this campaign on April 21, 1918, soon to be replaced by a fool named Hermann Göring.

And equally symbolic was the fact that the famed Red Baron died disillusioned with this war. He had killed eighty enemy pilots, but he didn't see any meaning in that. There would always be more pilots to kill, but what did the killing achieve? It merely helped other Germans to advance a few yards over torn territory that no one wanted.

Some people, especially the Americans, insisted on seeing the Red Baron as a romantic, an image manifested years later by Charles Schulz, the creator of the *Peanuts* comic strip, who would develop a storyline in which the dog Snoopy went after the Red Baron. But such things were fantasies. The Red Baron was simply a powerful killing machine who broke down in 1918. And he did not even die in direct combat. A stray bullet, perhaps fired by one particular Canadian, killed him on the spot. And like many others, he could not be replaced.

With insufficient supplies and undernourished horses, the German infantry still made real advances in this last campaign. But Ludendorff had trouble sending up munitions and food. His trucks had iron wheels because rubber was scarce in Germany, and inevitably these wheels cut the roads to mud and dust. The supply line of the German Army was beginning to wear out.

The elite units did well, early on. But when the experienced spearhead troops got butchered and could not be replaced, the German effort lessened, then stopped.

In this new offensive, the Germans were advancing over more and more territory already ravaged by the war. As they came over the sites of previous battles, they entered a wilderness of shattered skeletons, broken equipment, and rusty barbed wire, a junkyard of a landscape. There was no way advancing soldiers could imagine any value in dying for this pathetic stretch of earth, this same stretch for which their brothers had died to no end over the last two years. Why die to claim a ruined land?

In this blood-drenched year of 1918, Ludendorff's spring offensive reduced German forces from 5,100,000 to 4,200,000. Such losses were unthinkable. It was worse than Verdun. For Germany to lose 278,000 dead at Verdun was agony. But now Ludendorff was surpassing that, with no results.

Then, on August 8, 1918, the morale of the German Army collapsed. Vast numbers of retreating German troops began to mock advancing German soldiers because they were seen as prolonging the war. Shouts rang out:

"Scabs!"

"Strikebreakers!"

"What do you think you are fighting for?"

The British were now attacking with more tanks than ever before in history. These machines came to the front on trains in huge containers printed with the deceptive words "water tank," and this is where the name *tank* came from. At the beginning of the war they were an experiment. But now the British saw that these machines could break through the trenches and the barbed wire and that they terrified even the bravest German soldiers.

Meanwhile the Yanks were coming. At Belleau Wood and Château-Thierry, these brash young soldiers surged, making fast frontal assaults, disregarding all costs. The verve of the boys was legendary. At Château-Thierry the US force broke through the entire enemy line. At another point an amazing marine sergeant, a gunner who already had two medals of honor, shouted to his troops: "Come on, you sons of bitches! Do you want to live forever?"

At another place, a cheerful Tennessee trooper named Sergeant Alvin York made history. As a poor boy in Tennessee, he went hunting every day to get food for his family's table, and he knew more about shooting turkeys than almost anyone else. When he and his five soldiers were surrounded by 154 German troops, they killed twenty-two men on the spot, and the other 132, stunned, all surrendered. The surrendering German lieutenant, looking at York's half dozen, stammered, "Are these all the men you have?"

York, the best shot in the army, became a legend, and people named streets after him, like York Avenue in Manhattan. York could not understand the fuss and said that shooting Germans was like shooting turkeys. Probably it was.

Other notable Americans did heroic work too. Jess Fixom, a Cherokee warrior, went through the woods and ambushed untold numbers of enemy troops. A Lakota warrior, Joseph Cloud, promised that he would scalp any enemy soldier, or as he phrased it, he would "lift any German's hair." Impressive above all were the Pawnees, who ravaged the German lines and died at a rate fourteen times that of other American soldiers. Choctaws and other Native Americans, using twenty-six different languages, relayed sensitive information over field telephones, translating *casualties* as *scalps* and *machine guns* as *guns that shoot fast*. These were the first of the famed Code Talkers. German linguists failed to make sense of what these heroes were saying. Even if they had spoken the languages, they could never have understood references to "grains of corn" (that is, hand grenades) or the "mother gun who roars" (heavy artillery).

The French president, Georges Clemenceau, invited these heroes into the presidential palace and gave them glittering medals, kisses on both cheeks, and endless toasts of wine, and then declared that these were the true sons of the American West.

In some French sectors, the Americans became legends. The superb American general John Pershing led a division of American troops to liberate the town of Saint-Mihiel. Enduring fearful losses in a frontal assault, the Americans shattered the German line. People did not know what to make of this first captain from West Point, who wore no medals and who insisted, to the fury of many, that black troops were equal to white troops. A few swinish critics called him "Nigger Jack," a name that his men spun into a positive nickname, Black Jack. His men adored him and would follow him through the gates of hell. Many believed he was the best US soldier since Ulysses S. Grant.

Pershing led his advancing troops into Saint-Mihiel, a town that had been degraded for three miserable years by the meanest German troops. Many of those troops had forced the women of the town to repeatedly have sex with them, in exchange for food for their starving families. Rarely were Germans hated more than here. Now, when Pershing led his soldiers into town as liberators, he was overwhelmed by weeping crowds of grateful Frenchwomen. Girls, sobbing, kissed these liberators and declared that they had never seen men so magnificent.

Pershing beamed. "We gave 'em a darned good licking, didn't we?" he laughed, in a comment widely publicized. But he did not kiss any of these women because he was in love with a female artist hidden in Paris, a lovely twenty-three-year-old blonde who spoke little English and had trouble pronouncing the name Pershing, so she decided to call him "General Darling." But Pershing's men did kiss these willing women, again and again, until everyone lost count.

The women of France loved these Americans, and Pershing was proud. Many soldiers watched an old lady, holding a crucifix in her hands on a bit of string, as she walked up to one Yank. She put the cross round his neck and made him a promise. "My son," she smiled, "you shall not die."

Pershing, who had lost his wife and daughters a couple of years before in a tragic fire and who had been mourning far too long, loved this moment and laughed for the first time in a long while.

The pain in Ludendorff was as great as the joy in Pershing. On August 8 he finally understood that he was losing the war, and he fell to the floor in his headquarters. His mouth foaming, he screamed like a wounded beast. He later wrote of this as "the Black Day of the German Army" and was enraged to find that, as he saw it, his people were failing him. If they had tried harder, he insisted, they would have done better, and they would have won, even against the 1,000,000,000 people he had lined up against them.

Ludendorff did not understand that it was his fault that Germany was at war with 1,000,000,000 people. However, he did understand that his military effort was collapsing. So he screamed and fell. His staff closed the door and summoned his psychiatrist.

Of course they kept most people from hearing about this. The screaming and the foaming at the mouth would not be believable if it were not attested by multiple sources. But did it mean that Ludendorff was getting crazier? Or is it possible that he was now less crazy? Some might guess that this collapse happened because he had finally seen things as they were and he realized that he was losing a world war.

Indeed he was losing the world.

For a man who dreamed that he would surpass Napoleon and make his army the supreme military power, this descent from the sublime to the ridiculous was dizzying. It reminds a historian of Napoleon himself, who entered Russia with 400,000 men and who came out with 30,000. Indeed, only Napoleon had failed as much as Ludendorff. As disasters, the two men were walking monuments.

The Germans were still fighting, but their spark was fading. And word was spreading through the ranks that Americans were willing to let any enemy soldier surrender, that the concept of a soldier's right to surrender was universal among these troops no matter how much they hated an enemy. The idea now spread among the German troops, as if they were saying, "Let's surrender to the Americans. Let's get it over with."

More than 100,000 Americans—often two or three times that number—were arriving every month. Will Rogers quipped, "Germany couldn't figure out how America could get troops over there and get them trained so quick. They didn't know that in our manual there is nothing about *retreating*, and when you only got to teach an army to go one way, you do it in half the time." President Wilson loved this remark and repeated it. Americans were reminded of the "Battle Hymn of the Republic" which promised to blow the trumpet "that shall never call retreat."

American troops were eager, and they worried only that the Germans might surrender before the Americans taught them a lesson. Soldiers of the American Army then began to do something strange and awesome. They began to desert, but in a way never done before: They "deserted to the front," moving ahead of their chums, looking for any movement they could join, any squad going forward, to send at least one German to hell.

Soon observers were saying of the Germans, "For the first time they are on the defensive." "These Germans are not the soldiers they used to be." "Their defeat is just a matter of time."

German troops, who had been told of the ineptitude of Yanks, were surprised. A corporal named Recklinghausen was blunt. "If those Americans in front of us are reliable examples of the average American troops coming here, and if there are as many of them as they say, then it is Goodbye for all of us."

Worse, the Yanks dropped telling leaflets over No Man's Land. Read one: "Your fight is hopeless. America will cook your goose. Your submarines are of no use. We are making more ships than you are sinking. Your trade is destroyed. . . . Germany's industries are going under."

The Americans were not the only heroes. The British had incredibly glorious moments too, staggering successes that somehow made up for the painful stalemates of the past. At the Battle of Amiens, the British Fourth Army captured 13,000 prisoners. They moved so fast that one squad surrounded German officers while they were having breakfast. Elsewhere, British tanks hit in large numbers, at multiple points of impact, so swiftly that the Germans could not react promptly, and soon the German offensive began to recede, until their soldiers were back where they had started, but with 1,000,000 casualties lost, fine fellows whom they had lost in Ludendorff's go-for-broke extravaganza.

What could a German think of the promises that Ludendorff had made, that America could not raise an army in time? What to make of his proud words, "I don't give two hoots for the American

Army?" Ludendorff's poor troops had done well, if one considers that they lacked enough planes, enough trucks with tires, enough healthy horses, enough fodder and food, enough bandages, and enough medicine. But they had failed. Worse, they had lost more than the Allies. Where was the victory he promised? Was it possible that the Battle of Annihilation would annihilate the German Army that Ludendorff saw as the best on Earth?

Ludendorff had no explanations and no replacements. His situation was a horror. His home front was starving. His allies were deserting. His troops were infected with influenza, not to mention pacifism. Meanwhile, Americans were coming in force, the British tanks were upsetting all plans, the German Navy was in revolt, and the German Army's desertions were sky high. The situation was dire. After Ludendorff's offensive, the German Army was so battered that it could not advance anywhere. It could only try to defend itself.

Interestingly, German records from this time henceforth stopped making reference to advancing. To use a phrase from ancient Rome, the word became conspicuous by its absence.

Ludendorff prepared a report for his Kaiser giving a positive spin to each of these disasters. He argued that the Ludendorff Offensive had been impressive and had battered the Allies to the core. He argued that it was not what it appeared. Alas, this was rot. The offensive caused horrific losses that no German could make good and achieved no objective that any could see.

With their new advantage, the Allied leaders now began to discuss what kind of peace they would offer Germany. Unfortunately for Ludendorff, they wanted to give Germany the same murderous peace that Ludendorff had inflicted on the Russians. And it got worse. In England, Prime Minister Lloyd George declared that German leaders should be tried for their crimes. The word *genocide* did not exist. It would be coined to describe German conduct in the *next* war, in 1943, by a Jew in New York, one Raphael Lemkin, who was expert in studying the German way of war. But the drift toward genocide was visible in 1918. Lloyd George wanted to summon German leaders the way ancient Romans had summoned barbarians and make them give an account of themselves. He estimated that Britain should try 1,000 of these barbarians at war's end in Westminster Hall.

Meanwhile Germany was crumbling. German soldiers—soldiers Ludendorff needed—were deserting by the thousands every day. Railroad workers were declaring that they wanted to stop troop trains from bringing reinforcements to the front. Mutiny was in the air, and some divisions were talking of not advancing at all. And there was only a few days' worth of food left at the front for the troops.

In Berlin depressing reports came out that the government would have to cut rations yet again, even though the average German was now receiving only enough food for a two-year-old child.

And there was worse news. Ludendorff's allies began to talk of a separate peace. Austria and Bulgaria warned Ludendorff that they could fight only a little longer—they said they could not make war after November. The German people wondered how long this could go on. Would Germany exist as a nation after the New Year?

Ludendorff's wife experienced terrible losses. Over the previous two years, her two sons in the air force had been killed in Ludendorff's offensives. The details of their deaths are heartbreaking. On September 5, 1917, Margarethe's son Lieutenant Franz

Pernet of the Jasta Boelcke Aviation group went up in the skies to fight the Allies. Two of his friends had died the previous month, and he was grim. He was brave, but he was facing formidable Allied pilots who were better trained and had machines that flew circles around him. Just before going up, the boy wrote home: "Mother, you cannot imagine what a heavenly feeling it is when all the day's fighting is successfully over, to lie in bed and say to oneself before going to sleep, 'Thank God! You have another twelve hours to live!'"

Franz was young, short, and little, with more spunk than experience. A small girl in a park had said that he, such a young fellow in uniform, looked like her postman. And now, on this fated day, Ludendorff sent him up from the Dutch coast against a New Zealand pilot named Keith Park.

This was murderous bad luck. Park was one of the best pilots in the world. Two decades later he would be the top airman defending London against Hitler, in the most successful air campaign in British history. One day in August 1940, his men would knock down sixty-nine German planes in a single day. Nothing could stop this man.

And now Park came upon Ludendorff's son. The two squared off for a moment, and then Park did something mysterious, which eyewitnesses could not quite explain. In seconds, Park shifted and was behind the boy, and then he fired five bursts, which tore through the boy's craft like shrapnel through paper.

The boy fell like a dying bird. He was twenty-two. His flying career had lasted twelve weeks.

When Margarethe received the news of her son's death, she let out a cry like a wounded animal. Later she wrote that she lived through that moment again and again "as if in a dream." She suffered more when she received the last letter that the boy had written, which was so full of spunk and spirit, and which reminded her of the magnificent fellow he had been.

Later, on March 22, 1918, at the height of the Ludendorff Offensive, another of Margarethe's sons, Erich, went up in his plane and tried to fight. Erich was a sincere and handsome boy. His mother said he was "tall and slender, by far the best looking of my boys." He was the most intelligent too and had the brains to sense that he was doomed. Just before dying, during a leave home on his birthday, he said gently, "Mother, you mustn't be sad. Remember that I love my profession with my whole heart, and although I have gone through a good deal, I wouldn't have missed a moment of this year."

In passion Erich was superior to most officers. He hoped to become a general. People thought his advances came because he was Ludendorff's son, but they came because of his merits. He never received favoritism and he was an impeccable officer.

Erich had the misfortune to fly against a British pilot named Thomas Sydney Sharpe of the RFC 73 Squadron from Gloucester, England, who already had six kills to his credit. Sharpe was a rising expert—he had won his six kills in one month—and now he descended upon the boy from "out of the sun"—that is, positioned so that sunlight was in the boy's eyes. Half blinded, the boy had a difficult time defending himself, and Sharpe tore him apart.

Erich's body washed up on the Dutch coast. Ludendorff put both bodies in the morgue and visited them again and again. For some reason he delayed the process of sending them home. He wrote a strange letter to his wife saying that it felt good to visit the dead boys. Finally he had them moved to a posh crypt in the Kaiser Wilhelm Memorial Church in Berlin. But that was all he could do. He could not think of anything more. In the next war, Allied bombers would obliterate the church and the boys would be dust in the wind.

After Ludendorff killed her boys, his wife grew distant. From this time she wore black and never smiled. The death of her second son, soon after the first, was too much. In her memoir she wrote, "I felt the full force of the blow. I do not know what happened. I only know that I collapsed and from that day, for years, I was always sick and sorry." Slowly the beautiful woman drifted into melancholy, and then into morphine. Life was not supposed to turn out this way. She had had such dreams. She was the kind of old-fashioned German woman for whom family was everything . . . and now she was losing everything, to her husband, the general.

So Ludendorff lost his family and his war at the same time. He took some real comfort, however, that it was not his fault. Like the Kaiser, and later like Hitler, he convinced himself that Germans were failing *him* and not the other way around.

Churchill said that in this war Germany had but one way out. It could call for a conciliatory peace without annexations and indemnities, in which everyone would just cease fighting and go home. That offer, Churchill said, would have been irresistible to most people in every Allied nation.

Or Ludendorff could do something base. He could become savage, ruthless. He could declare the Germans to be right, he could seek scapegoats to punish for the disasters he himself had caused, and he could then escalate the war to the point of agony in the hope that the Allied nations would collapse and sue for peace.

It was a choice between honor and paranoia. He could admit that his armies had lost a world war, with millions of lives squandered in his meaningless battles, and then he could ask for peace, a peace of the brave, a peace without victors.

Or Ludendorff could blame others for the disasters he had created, demand victory against the 1,000,000,000 people arrayed against Germany, and then escalate the war to the level of an apocalypse.

CHAPTER 9

Ludendorff Loses the World War and Blames the Jews

W ALTER RATHENAU WAS the son of a prominent Jewish businessman who had founded Allgemeine Elektricitäts-Gesellschaft (General Electricity Company), or AEG. During World War I, he convinced the War Ministry to set up the Raw Materials Department, in which he would hold senior positions. He was vital to Germany's war effort, leading the way in both developing raw materials threatened by the British blockade and using materials captured from occupied Belgium and France. But his patriotic service to Germany would be no protection from the rise of anti-Semitism in the years to come.

Despite the heroic efforts of men like Rathenau to feed materials and supplies to the German military, they could not withstand the endless demands of Ludendorff's war. Back in the United States, more and more men were volunteering. The most popular man in America, Teddy Roosevelt, had lost his boy Quentin in aerial combat against the Germans, and Roosevelt was doing his all to drum up support for enlistments, probably out of a desire to give meaning to the boy's death.

Quentin, a boy with bad eyes and a bad back, would never have been drafted. But he pulled every string his family possessed to enlist in the Air Corps. He did not think it right to stay out of the war at a posh place like Harvard, with his multimillionaire fiancée Edith Whitney, while others did their part. Quentin's father got him into a splendid flying squadron, where his spunk and courage earned him countless friends. But they said he was too brave, like his father, and they worried that he took risks too willingly.

In his first month at the front he shot down his first German craft, and that was fine. But next month he saw seven German planes when he was alone. He attacked and took two bullets in the face. His plane crashed in seconds. His career as an airman had lasted eight weeks.

The servants at the White House were devastated. The Secret Service remembered fondly how as a boy, he and his friends, who called themselves the White House Gang, would ambush them with snowballs on many an occasion, and they never could see where the snowballs were coming from.

One guard remembered how Quentin was worried over the morale of a sick brother and how he enlisted the staff to cheer up the boy. Together they got the family's pet pony, Algonquin, onto the elevator and brought the horse into the boy's bedroom, to give him an unexpected surprise.

Another guard remembered how Quentin as a young boy formed a friendship with a staff member's child and did not care that the boy was black. That today would be unsurprising. But in the early part of the twentieth century, when blacks were seen as mere animals, that was unprecedented. Quentin did not see race anywhere. He always wished the world well. Quentin's death roused

Roosevelt. A hero from the Spanish-American War, Roosevelt now traveled across America, drumming up support.

Desperate to circumvent backlash, the German government tried to put a positive spin on the death of the boy and detailed 1,000 troops to give a funeral with honors to Roosevelt's son. They wrote an unctuous proclamation to salute the boy's glorious death. But then an obscure German soldier spoiled everything. He took a photo of the dead boy, sprawled in agony beside his crumpled plane, and turned the photo into a postcard, which he sold everywhere at great profit. People in the Allied nations were startled by the spectacle of this man's making money from the suffering of a dead boy. And the American people were especially enraged.

In 1918, this last year of the war, Ludendorff lost more than 1,000,000 men. This included countless deserters hiding in the forests or escaping to the Netherlands. This included suicides on the field of battle. This included boys who went insane and had to be committed. Germans in many sectors said life was "horrors without end," and pacifists suggested that this was worse than having "an end with horrors." Food was becoming so scarce that new recruits, reporting to the army for training, often fainted during the first day's maneuvers.

The German Navy, which had helped bring about this war by alarming the British with its growing size and with its admirals' aggressive statements, was close to mutiny. Terrible rumors that gloomy German admirals might send the navy out to sea to fight the British in one desperate last battle swept the fleet. The sailors wanted nothing to do with a match against a naval force they considered the best in the world. Seditious sailors wrote a manifesto that declared, "The launching of the fleet is to be prevented." Sailors knew what would happen if they attacked the British Navy.

Meanwhile, the British blockade, tightening like a python, was crushing Germany, keeping out food and matériel. Germany could not cope much longer. Ludendorff had drafted too many farmers, had confiscated too many chemicals needed for fertilizer, and killed too many of Germany's sons in his offensives. The farms were dying.

The German Air Force had gone from the best in Europe to being almost insignificant. The German armies had been good and had defeated the Russians, but only the Russians. That victory brought no real triumph. The treaty at Brest won Germany multiple spoils, but Ludendorff couldn't collect them. The signing of the treaty released some German units to the West, but they were surly and unreliable. Meanwhile, Lenin's men were spreading Communist propaganda throughout Eastern Europe.

Ludendorff's best shock troops, who had gone forward bravely in his last offensive, were now dead, and they were the last of the best. The surviving German troops were now terrorized by the new British tanks, especially the light Whippet tanks, which were swift and hard to hit. Ludendorff tried to tell his artillerists to stand firm and smash those tanks with cannon fire, but his brave soldiers ran at the sight of these beasts. Soon his troops began to hallucinate over tanks and to imagine they heard them coming, even where they did not exist.

Some soldiers borrowed an American word to describe the tanks and called them ironsides, and they said the word with awe. These tanks were like the fabled American warships of the early 1800s, made of that special oak that grew on islands off Virginia. The wood was so hard that cannonballs bounced off it. At least one such ship, thus protected, was nicknamed Old Ironsides, and it is a splendid sight in Boston Harbor today. These new ironsides, these tanks, were just as impressive.

German factory workers tried to produce their own tanks, but the process was slow. They had trouble making engines that were powerful enough and steel plate that was strong enough. And the production managers could not make sense of Ludendorff's contradictory demands. Just how many tanks did Ludendorff really need? How fast, how small, how thick? And how many submarines did he want? How much artillery? Ludendorff's demands for one meant less steel for another. And Ludendorff wanted so much of everything. His beloved Paris Gun consumed 250 tons of steel, and it accomplished nothing. That same steel could have produced so many tanks, all desperately needed. But his men could not convince Ludendorff of things like this.

On paper, things were not hopeless. No foreign soldier stood on German soil. No German army had been entirely defeated. But ever since the ultimate failure of the Ludendorff Offensives, the Germans could only wait. The enemy could maneuver, and Ludendorff could not. The enemy could fight at the place of its choosing, and Ludendorff could not. This is why Ludendorff did not move forward on any occasion after the Ludendorff Offensives. Simply stated, the enemy could do anything unexpected, and Ludendorff could only wait.

Famed military historian Hans Delbrück said that the fault was Ludendorff's alone. "He could not adapt himself to feasible objectives and thus he rendered the soldiers' heroism null and void." Delbrück became an enemy of Ludendorff and eventually had to leave the country because he told inconvenient truths, especially in his articles for the press. His prime accusation was that Ludendorff and Hindenburg blindly pursued military victory without making a single long-term objective.

Every day brought worse news, and soon Ludendorff's staff sensed he was afraid to attend the morning briefings for fear of hearing bad tidings. Operations were down, as Ludendorff's troops paused to loot the warehouses and even to surrender to the enemy. Large units sometimes did not return, and stories drifted back of mass desertions, of one hundred soldiers surrendering to a single American private.

An exception to this bad news was the story of Lance Corporal Adolf Hitler, who was evacuated from the western front to a German military hospital in Pomerania after being partly blinded by a British mustard gas attack. As he recuperated, he wanted only to return to battle. But the enthusiasm of men like young Hitler was rare by October 1918. There were so few like him.

Ludendorff's foreign enemies were winning, and he was becoming paranoid. As he studied the vaunted Schlieffen Plan, based on Hannibal's victory at Cannae, he came to identify with the star-crossed Hannibal, who, he asserted, was betrayed by his own people. Ludendorff felt he had the same unappreciated genius as Hannibal. And he began to seek scapegoats to blame for what was happening. One day he was disgusted with the Catholics or the Masons. The next day it was the Socialists or the Communists. Then he was grumbling about the Kaiser or the government or the war profiteers or the women at the home front. And always he blamed the Jews.

The Allies were making plans for a march on Berlin. American president Woodrow Wilson was talking about "peace without victory," but it was a peace that Ludendorff found problematic. Wilson wanted a kind peace, similar to the one given in 1865 to

Confederate soldiers like his father, who had been an officer in the Civil War. Wilson wanted a peace without brutal reprisals.

But even the gentle Wilson understood the deviousness of German militarists like Ludendorff, and he was insisting that the Germans first prove their sincerity. He wanted the Germans to immediately withdraw from *all* occupied territory, including Alsace and Lorraine, and Belgium and Poland, just for peace negotiations to *begin*. And he wanted the German Navy and Air Force to give up large numbers of ships and planes so that the Germans could not emerge again as a major power if the truce should break down. The last thing he wanted was to give the Germans a breathing space, after which they could launch the war anew.

Wilson insisted also that he would negotiate only with true representatives of the German people, and he challenged the right of Ludendorff, Hindenburg, and the Kaiser to speak for anyone. President Wilson wanted this war, the worst in history, to end definitively. He did not want a peace parley to be a ruse that would allow a rested Germany to fight again.

To Ludendorff these American demands were crushing—and these were the demands made by the more liberal Americans. Other Americans were more severe. The top American general, "Black Jack" Pershing, wrote to the Allied Supreme War Council and urged that the Germans be forced to sign an unconditional surrender. Former president Teddy Roosevelt in similar fashion demanded that the Allies march on Berlin and beat the Germans to the ground. He wanted them to be smashed so that they would know they were whipped. Only then, he said, should America make peace.

Many French leaders agreed. General Charles Mangin, "the Butcher," endorsed this strategy. Marshal Ferdinand Foch, who had been appointed commander of the Allied armies, wanted the peace terms to be so severe that Germany could never hurt its neighbors again.

Their call for a march on Berlin was compelling. If they had done this, German officers would never have been able to convince their people that they had been undefeated. This could have defeated all Nazi pretenses and stopped their coming to power. And this in turn could easily have prevented World War II.

Meanwhile, Ludendorff was losing his nerve. He understood how bad things were. By September 28, 1918, Ludendorff was running out of options. Only now did the defeated soldier admit that an armistice was necessary, adding frantically that it had to be sought "at once." And like a fox, he demanded that it be done by the politicians and not the generals. This way he was shifting responsibility for the lost war onto the government.

By October 2 Ludendorff had convinced his chief to assent to this strategy and declare, regarding the need for peace, that "the Army cannot wait 48 hours." Evidently Ludendorff feared that his army would collapse before peace was established. If that happened, he would be blamed for losing the war.

By this time Americans were present on the battlefields of Europe in such numbers, and German soldiers were deserting in such equal numbers, that Ludendorff decided he needed a vote of confidence of some kind. On October 26, Ludendorff offered his resignation to the Kaiser in the royal palace in Berlin, assuming that the pathetic man would reject it, as was his custom. But now, in the midst of these disasters, the Kaiser surprised him. This time the Kaiser accepted the offer. And to his astonishment, his friend Hindenburg raised no objection. Ludendorff stormed out, with

Hindenburg following silently. As they left, the Kaiser muttered with pleasure, "I have separated the Siamese Twins."

Outside, Hindenburg tried to offer Ludendorff a ride, but the angry general grumbled that he was going away on leave. Hindenburg told Ludendorff that he could not depart—he would have to stay and brief his successor regarding papers, personnel, and procedures. Otherwise he was decapitating the entire headquarters. Ludendorff answered that one of the subordinates, a lieutenant general named Hermann von Kuhl, could take over, and he stomped off like an angry child.

Ludendorff went home to his wife, pale and exhausted, and sank into his favorite armchair, fuming. His wife tried to draw him out, but he only brooded, and then he jumped up and shouted, "In two weeks we shall have no Empire and no Kaiser, you'll see!"

On the boulevards people met him with withering stares. In the theaters, audiences cheered when they announced his departure. At the local symphony the audience applauded his resignation. At home the neighbors told his wife they wanted them gone. Crank phone calls came in the night, threatening them. Obviously their days were numbered.

Some people in Germany loved Ludendorff. The top-level Junker elites, the presidents of the corporations, the millionaires and the plutocrats, and the people he had enriched and flattered all liked him and felt that he had their interests at heart, as indeed he did. But the German people at large, the middle and lower middle class of people, whose sons he had slaughtered on too many battlefields, saw him as a predator.

Ludendorff, afraid, ran away from home. He secreted himself in an unlisted apartment, where he was silent for days. He bought a disguise, blue sunglasses and a blond wig, and then made plans to leave Germany. Within moments he had gone from being the leader of one of the great armies of the world to being a pariah whom the mob wanted to lynch.

In England, Prime Minister Lloyd George talked again of putting the German leaders on trial. Lloyd George wanted Ludendorff and his kind in the docket, to be judged by English law. Some would be put to death, and this would certainly include anyone at the top, like Ludendorff. If he came to trial, he would die.

Ludendorff had much blood on his hands. The Belgians remembered an operation code-named Alberich, which took place in the winter of 1917. Ludendorff's troops had forced 500,000 civilian laborers to work for months building fortifications near the French–Belgian border, which the West called the Hindenburg Line. These laborers worked feverishly unloading 1,250 trainloads of materials and built a huge continuous fortification of concrete and reinforced steel, behind which the Germans then retreated. During this retreat, they destroyed massive stretches of Belgian and French railroads, orchards, and mines. They confiscated locomotives, leveled towns, emptied factories, poisoned wells, slaughtered cattle, and even blew craters in the center of crossroads, leaving behind women and children with scant rations.

And there was more. Ludendorff had planted countless booby traps: explosive devices hidden in barrels of flour, inside sides of ham, and under pillows and mattresses. Most devilish were those placed inside pianos. The moment one played a particular key, the piano detonated. Ludendorff pretended that his measures targeted the military, but this was rot. Soldiers on military campaigns are not known for stopping to play the piano. Ludendorff was killing civilians too.

He had stripped many Belgian factories of their equipment, making them hollow. He had flooded mines. He had torn up railroad tracks and stolen more than 90 percent of the locomotives. Belgium, which had been one of the top ten economies of the world, was so crippled that it would never regain its full prominence and would be a backwater for decades.

In retreat, Rupprecht, crown prince of Bavaria, commander of the German Sixth Army, and one of the few royals who had a solid education, had condemned Ludendorff for insisting on "the destruction of all highroads, villages, towns and wells." Vineyards and gardens and green mountains had been turned into a wilderness of barbed wire and dead trees. Valleys were turned into open sewers. And here Prince Rupprecht intervened. He begged Ludendorff to stop, and in particular he pleaded that Ludendorff spare the castle of Coucy, a fortress of the thirteenth century that no longer had military importance. Coucy was one of the sublime works of the Middle Ages, with the largest castle keep in Europe.

Angrily, Ludendorff ignored Rupprecht and stuffed the castle with twenty-eight tons of explosives, then blew it to heaven in March of 1917. He said the towering structure might be used as a military observation post. Interestingly, this was the identical vapid justification that the German Army used to destroy the Cathedral of Reims.

In April 1917, the French government declared the ruined edifice at Coucy "a monument to barbarity." Herbert Hoover, the American engineer leading the humanitarian relief efforts in Belgium, declared Ludendorff an abomination. He swore he could prove it in court.

And these atrocities by Ludendorff were merely over a two-month period. Ludendorff had done many similar campaigns at other times in the war. The extent of these crimes together has caused scholars, like Dr. Jeff Lipkes of Cornell University, to suggest that Ludendorff's work in Belgium was a rehearsal for Germany's genocidal work in Europe during the next war. Lipkes's book on Ludendorff's abominations in Belgium during the First World War is 815 pages long and is aptly titled *Rehearsals*. Published by the University of Louvain Press, *Rehearsals* describes how Ludendorff destroyed much of that nation in the name of a superior civilization that he pretended to be bringing to the world. Lipkes argues that what we call Nazi and associate with Hitler was started years before by Ludendorff and his ilk.

Professor Isabel V. Hull, also of Cornell University, thinks that talking about Ludendorff's work as genocidal "is going a little too far." She notes that Ludendorff and his cadre did not consciously want to eliminate the Belgians as a people, and therefore we cannot call their work genocidal.

Others do not concur. US ambassador Samantha Power, who has studied and worked on genocide both at Harvard and the United Nations, concludes that many genocidal processes may be conducted by people who are not *consciously* trying to eliminate a particular nation, and she cites events in Rwanda as an example. For her the issue is whether there is savage destruction, on a scale above civilized limits, sufficient to cripple a people. If so, then the effort is genocidal. And on that basis, the work of Ludendorff in Belgium was arguably genocidal.

When the war began four years earlier, General Baron von Marschall had had a premonition that "Ludendorff would wage war until the last ounce of strength was pumped from the German people . . . and then the monarchy would bear the blame."

Another general issued a similar warning to General Falkenhayn: "Ludendorff would end by driving Germany to Revolution." It is difficult to say that these men were wrong.

The Kaiser was blamed for many of Ludendorff's crimes, and perhaps this was unfair. The Kaiser's generals frequently kept him in the dark and fed him only the information they wanted him to hear. The Kaiser maintained his innocence and told journalists how he had tried to fight decently. He insisted he had not committed any crimes. Yet he *had* allowed evil to be done in the name of his throne. Just once, years later, the Kaiser dropped his guard. When signing a photograph of himself, he wrote these chilling words on the picture: *Was it all wrong?*

Perhaps it was. After the war was over, he said he wished he had gone off in 1918 at the head of his troops and died in battle. That way, he felt, his ancestors would have been proud. Instead he wavered, like a gloomy Hamlet in the wings of his castle, and did nothing.

Meanwhile, somebody had to sign the peace that would end the war. The politicians of Germany eventually sent a delegation to Allied headquarters in France to discuss the terms. And the German delegates knew they would have to sign and bear the guilt of being the ones who negotiated Germany's failure. Ludendorff had seen to that.

The shame from the German side was huge. They had to sign an 80,000-word document that blamed them for Ludendorff's abominations in the war. But at least the German armies were allowed to march home, where their officers were allowed to brag that they had not been beaten formally.

Shortly after, Ludendorff paid a visit to the British Embassy in Berlin and conferred with General Sir Neill Malcolm, the chief military attaché. Ludendorff went into a rant about how he and his army had been mistreated by his government in the last days of the war, just when they were winning. Painfully the British general tried to make sense of these confused assertions. Malcolm, in fluent German, asked Ludendorff a single question: "Do you mean, General, that you were stabbed in the back?"

Ludendorff seized the phrase. "Stabbed in the back?" he snapped, eyes flashing. "Yes, that's it exactly. We were stabbed in the back."

Malcolm was using a phrase that had been made popular by George Bernard Shaw in 1916, but these words had a special resonance in Germany, the nation that celebrated the myth of Siegfried, the knight stabbed in the back by an evil spirit named Hagen. Ludendorff, who saw himself as a mythic hero, now had his mantra, which he soon was repeating to anyone who would listen, a phrase that for him summed up the tragedy of Germany: "As a British general has rightly said, the German Army was stabbed in the back."

Malcolm denied this. He said he had merely engaged in what Proust called indirect discourse—that is, stating a man's position from the man's vantage point. And when Ludendorff pretended that Malcolm had said that the German Army had been stabbed in the back, the Englishman wrote powerful denials, saying that he had never endorsed the stab-in-the-back legend. Interestingly, the German press refused to print Malcolm's denials. Swiftly, Germans seized on the legend because it was convenient. Superpatriots could now argue that traitorous politicians had sabotaged the German Army at the vital moment when a glorious victory was almost assured. And everyone believed that Jews led the plot.

Ludendorff found that Germans were only mildly interested in hearing his tales about evil Catholics or Masons, or about dreadful Socialists or Communists. But he discovered an attentive and rabid audience the instant he described how Jews were causing Germany's time of troubles. No matter that Rathenau, the top industrialist in Germany, was a Jewish patriot who had helped Ludendorff much during the war. No matter that this Jew was the main reason that Germany had been able to keep fighting the last two years of the conflict. People listened avidly when Ludendorff spoke of nightmarish Jewish plots. And every time he told these tales, he conjured up new details to excite his eager audience.

Ludendorff never explained why these Jews were destroying Germany. What did these schemers want? Who directed them, to what end? No one asked; no one wanted to know. It was enough that the famed Ludendorff was telling them what they wanted to hear, that the fault was not Germany's and not the army's. Instead these dreadful foreigners, the Jews, had caused Germany's ills.

The US representative to the Supreme War Council, General Tasker H. Bliss, watched this scapegoating with distress. Bliss, trained as a diplomat, was a scholar who could see dangers at an early stage. Starting in October of 1918, even before the war ended, he warned people that the German militarists were still in control and that if unchecked, they would ruin Europe.

This old general, a master linguist who had studied at the military schools of Germany, England, and France and who understood the dangers of certain military men, should have been heeded. He knew that Germans should have been tearing down the old military regime and building a new republican government to get beyond their past. Then he saw Ludendorff cleverly gaining sympathy for the German Army, teaching people to despise their new republic. Too many people were being taken in by Ludendorff's stab-in-the-back legend, and the disinformation could murder the new republic.

The attraction of Ludendorff's legend is best exemplified in how it impacted one particular German soldier. When Germany was forced to surrender, Lance Corporal Adolf Hitler, lying in a hospital bed, wrote bitterly in his memoirs about the soldiers whom these Jews had allegedly betrayed with their armistice. "Was it for this that these boys of 17 years had sunk into the mud of Flanders?" he wrote. "Was this the meaning of the sacrifice which the German mother made to the Fatherland when with sore heart she let her best-loved boys march off, never to see them again? Did all this happen only so a gang of wretched criminals could lay hands on the Fatherland?"

Hitler's words hold a key phrase—he was seeking "the meaning of the sacrifice." He was seeking a justification for the failed war that brought so much loss. Not finding this, he sought conspiracies to make sense of the confusion. He was seeking redemption, and not finding it, he sought scapegoats.

Hitler in his blindness soon imagined a reckoning to punish the guilty. He later said: "If at the beginning of the war and during the war, 12,000 or 15,000 of these Hebrew corrupters of the people had been held under poison gas, as happened to hundreds of thousands of our very best German workers in the field, then the sacrifice of millions at the Front would not have been in vain."

So to understand the Holocaust that Hitler enacted during World War II, one must probably turn to the legends that Ludendorff spread about World War I. To understand Hitler's myopia, one must understand the sources from which it came. Let us imagine that Hitler described his views in words like these, which are merely a blend of the thousands of words of abuse that he printed against an innocent people: *The Jews lost our war. Therefore they should die by poison gas, just as our heroes did on the field of battle. If we remove the Jews from our nation, if we hit the Jews with poison gas, if we purge their influence from our land, then we shall be stronger. We shall win the next war and redeem the sacrifices of so many millions.*

FOR OVER SIX months in 1918 and 1919, the civilians of the new German government were trying to negotiate their peace talks with the Allied Powers, and on June 28, 1919, they were finally presented with the terms of the Treaty of Versailles. It was not as brutal as the Treaty of Brest-Litovsk, which Ludendorff had inflicted on Russia. It did not take away a third of the defeated power's territory as Ludendorff tried to do at Brest. Nor did it incorporate tens of millions of unwilling people into another nation the way Ludendorff incorporated people into the Reich. It did not take the greater part of their iron and coal and railroads, and it did not dismember the defeated nation as Ludendorff did when he claimed vast parts of Ukraine, Belarus, Poland, and Russia.

But the treaty was severe. Germany was being held responsible for the war and was forced to pay damages. And most outrageous to many Germans was one American clause, Article 231, written by two American diplomats, John Foster Dulles and Norman Davis, which forced Germans to admit that they were responsible for all the damages that came from the war. As the article put it, "Germany accepts the responsibility . . . for causing all the loss and damage . . . as a consequence of the war."

The Americans were kind, however. After establishing the liability of Germany to pay reparations for the damages inflicted on the Allies in Article 231, they followed with Article 232, which lessened Germany's responsibilities: "Germany . . . would be asked only to pay for civilian damages." This referred to the German destruction of homes, villages, and personal possessions in France, Belgium, Poland, and Russia.

The Dulles family, especially John's sister, Eleanor, would insist ever after that the Americans were against indemnities as a rule and that these two articles, especially the second, were there to reduce the obligations of Germany to a tolerable level. It was a compromise. German elites, however, ignored the second article and clung to the first like grim death. As they sketched it, the Americans had drafted a monster clause, which made the treaty abominable and illegal. They claimed, even before they had to sign it, that decent Germans had to fight the treaty and, worse yet, they had to fight the republic that signed it. Immediately Article 231 gave reactionary Germans a rabid propaganda advantage. Germany could lie and portray itself as a victim.

But no German seems to have spent much time looking at the next clause, Article 232, which lessened more than half the financial burden of war guilt. John Foster Dulles was not the fool he was alleged to be, even though he took a pounding for his work on the treaty.

John Foster, incidentally, was the brother of Allen Dulles, the consul in Switzerland who turned down the meeting with Lenin because he had a date with a gorgeous woman. This same John Foster was a superlative and brainy public servant, and his war guilt clause was never the monstrosity that the Hitler types alleged.

But how could Dulles have known that those seventeen words on war guilt would be seized by the Germans and used to condemn the entire 80,000-word document—and the validity of the whole new government of Germany?

Will Rogers noted that the Treaty of Versailles was long but that "It had to be that long to tell the Germans what we thought of them." Then he added: "We could have settled the whole thing in one sentence: 'If you birds start anything again, we will give you the other barrel.'"

But few read the treaty all the way through, and this gave the extremists in Germany a propaganda opportunity. Rather than accepting blame for starting the war, rather than accepting responsibility for poison gas and unrestricted submarine war, rather than taking responsibility for the atrocities in Belgium, the Germans could now avoid these issues and pretend that the treaty was a Jewish abomination against the great German people, whose soldiers had fought nobly but who had been sabotaged by traitors just before they won a splendid victory.

They could also moan and groan that the indemnities that the treaty would inflict on Germany were so great they could not be paid. The great American financier Bernard Baruch was clear that they could be paid and indeed that they were not as awful as the colossal indemnities Ludendorff had demanded at Brest. But the Germans ignored Baruch, and some grumbled that the great man was a Jew and therefore unreliable.

So after Ludendorff demanded the armistice, he called it a crime. From the Kaiser down, a huge segment of German society agreed with Ludendorff's version of events. Eventually this view became nearly universal in Germany and Austria. At the war memorial at the University of Vienna, a visitor could soon see the statue of the noble soldier Siegfried, in bronze, stabbed in the back by the evil dwarf Hagen. It was a neat equation. Do you wish to be like the glorious knight or the evil dwarf? The question, phrased that way, was easy to answer.

At first it would be a challenge to get the people of Germany to believe this. But like monks chanting their prayers and mantras, the men in Ludendorff's circle found that if they repeated the stab-in-the-back legend enough, listeners would believe. As Irene Gunther wrote in her book *Nazi Chic*, "Those who chanted and echoed the 'stab in the back' legend again and again eventually convinced themselves[!] and others that the war, the hated Treaty [of Versailles], and the despised [Weimar] Republic, were all part of a vast worldwide Jewish conspiracy."

Gunther is wiser than she realizes when she notes that the early Nazis were convincing *themselves* by endless repetition.

Ludendorff knew that top Jews like Rathenau had fought for the fatherland to the end. He also knew that without this particular Jew, Germany would have collapsed years earlier. But Rathenau, now the minister of reconstruction of the new Weimar Republic, was insisting that Germany could fulfill its obligations under the treaty. This infuriated Ludendorff and other German nationalists, so he continued to complain that Germany had been stabbed in the back by Jews.

Ludendorff's stab-in-the-back legend did not just mean that generals like Ludendorff were blameless. It also meant that men like Ludendorff were to be followed. It also meant that the leaders of the new republic, like Rathenau, were evil and should be killed. It was no great leap from this lie to the conclusion that all Jews should be exterminated. German historian Holger Herwig said much when he asked: "Is it too far off the mark to suggest that the twisted road to Auschwitz began with the stab-in-the-back legend?"

So it was that this miserable war began with the Schlieffen Plan, which could not work, collapsed with the Ludendorff Offensive, which could not succeed, closed with the Versailles treaty, which could not be implemented, and culminated in a conspiracy legend against Jews, which could never be proven. A case can be made that the legends in which Ludendorff played a major and blood-drenched role would kill millions of Jews and Christians and would butcher European civilization for years to come. Indeed, they would cripple Europe for the better part of the twentieth century.

If Teddy Roosevelt's plan had prevailed and the Allied armies had gone all the way to Berlin, countless atrocities might have been avoided. Americans, who were the least weary of the Great Powers, could have led this march.

But Woodrow Wilson, jealous of Roosevelt's popularity, refused to make Roosevelt a general. Roosevelt could have carried the day, could have inspired the soldiers to win this last battle, and could have shattered Ludendorff's army in a true Battle of Annihilation. The Allied armies would have taken Berlin, and no rabid fool could have pretended, as Ludendorff and Hitler later did, that Germany had never been defeated.

THE LOSSES FROM World War I were huge. Imagine four long lines of men, walking at a medium pace in front of you, twenty-four hours a day, all year long, for four years, and that each man is walking to his death. In a single day on the Somme, the British lost 58,000 men. In the battle at Verdun, on both sides, 738,000 men were casualties. In just one battle in the Carpathian Mountains, the losses were 339,000 casualties total.

This war was so severe that nearly all the governments involved were overthrown. At the beginning of the war, all the nations in play except France were monarchies. At the end of the war, all the nations involved except Britain were republics. A book by Richard M. Watt summed up the damage with its title: *The Kings Depart.*

And depart they did. The Kaiser, unloved and frightened, left his nation for the Netherlands, which had remained neutral throughout the war. He escaped with forty-eight railway cars of luxuries and furniture, brought twenty-six servants and a court of forty-six, and enjoyed a bank account that today would be valued above $50,000,000. It was a court without a throne, but a court all the same. Nonetheless, he complained that he had barely enough to maintain his regal dignity.

His inner circle seems to have despised him. His valet left him after years of service. His youngest son, Joachim, committed suicide. With the shock of abdication and exile, his devoted wife, Augusta Victoria, who had stood with him through thick and thin, gave up and died.

A little boy wrote the Kaiser a letter on his birthday, saying how much he and his mother loved him: "I am only a little boy but I want to fight for you when I am a man. I am sorry because you are so terribly lonely. . . . There are so many little boys like me who love you." The Kaiser found the letter delightful and told the boy to visit him in the Netherlands anytime. The boy and his mother, Princess Hermione of Schoenaich-Carolath, did come to visit, and before long, the princess had entranced the Kaiser. She was nineteen years his junior and determined. Within months, she persuaded the

Kaiser to marry her. Though the princess was elegant, she also had appetites. She wanted to return in glory to Germany with the Kaiser and ascend the throne. She even coaxed the Kaiser to call her by a grand title, "Her Imperial and Royal Majesty, the German Queen of Prussia." She dreamed forever of returning to Germany in glory. In fact she did come back later, in 1945—and wound up ingloriously a prisoner in a Russian concentration camp.

The Kaiser's final years were a farce. He spent his time listening to his new wife telling him that his subjects were pigs for abandoning him. Still, the Kaiser was lucky to end this way. Most of the world blamed him for Ludendorff's atrocities and wanted him hanged. Many American songs written during the war years relayed this opinion: "We'll Hang Kaiser Billy from a Sour Apple Tree," "When the Yankees Yank the Kaiser off His Throne," "We'll Lick the Kaiser If It Takes Us Twenty Years," "I'd Like to See the Kaiser with a Lily in His Hand," and, a particular favorite, "The Kaiser Wants More Territory So We Shall Give Him Hell."

The American soldiers had meant it. The Kaiser was fortunate to escape. Other kings had less luck. Saddest was Nicholas II, the last czar of Russia. He and his family were summoned one night by drunken guards, who said they had orders to shoot him and his family then and there. His not-too-memorable last words were, "What? What?" And then they opened fire. The guards tried to shoot the whole family, including the four grand duchesses, but these young women were hiding so many jewels under their dresses that the bullets bounced off. The guards, confused by this apparently miraculous resistance, then chased the girls around the room and bayoneted each of them, one at a time, the poor girls screaming until they died, pinned to the floor like butterflies in a specimen box. It was a tragic end to a dynasty that went back three centuries.

Other dynasties died too—the house of Austria fell to dust, and so did that of Bulgaria, and more. Soon there were few dynasties left. When King Farouk was overthrown in Egypt, he said that eventually the world would have just five kings: "The king of diamonds, the king of clubs, the king of hearts, the king of spades, and the King of England."

But what did it all mean? It reminds the authors of the sarcastic quip by Voltaire on the worthless Battle of Bergen op Zoom of 1747, where 10,000 men died in the Netherlands for nothing: "What did it mean, I cannot see, but 'twas a famous victory."

Now in 1919, people felt that this war was a similar kind of rot, on a vaster scale. There had been endless murder, senseless slogans, and meaningless victories over too many years, all for nothing. And now there was nothing left.

One observer, George Kennan, the celebrated ambassador to Russia, called it a broken world and noted that the only thing that could express the damage and the disarray was the sound of a lonely saxophone echoing in the night. It was chaos.

But chaos offers opportunity. And in the lonely vacuum of this time, Ludendorff now worked to leave his mark and to prepare everyone for what he called "the next war," a war where Jews would be destroyed and where Germans would then achieve absolute victory.

CHAPTER 10

Ludendorff Moves to Murder the Jews and Fight a New War

O UR STORY SHOULD be over. After the damage Ludendorff did to the world during his war, he did not deserve another chapter in this life. But certain sectors of Germany seemed to need Ludendorff. Germany was a battered nation, and the people had lived for years under Ludendorff's relentless propaganda and had been hypnotized into believing his awesome versions of reality and his absurd promises of victory. They had been given a vision of a glorious future where, after ghastly sacrifice, they would live in a rich empire that even the British would envy. Now they awoke violently into a brave new world that had savage realities. Instead of victory they had defeat, and they owed reparations so severe that the future of the nation was said to be in doubt.

Many a German was at the end of his tether. Consider one deco-rated veteran walking the streets of Berlin. He had to sell his overcoat. He had been eating in the soup kitchens. He had been going to the municipal showers for delousing. He got small change by begging. He painted pretty postcards for tourists, but there were few tourists to buy them. This poor veteran was Adolf Hitler, a miserable man with faded dreams. A few writers have suggested he may have been brain damaged in the war. What is certain is that the only positive things he remembered about his youth were the friendships he had made with his fellow soldiers, those special moments of camaraderie and hope. There were millions like him. And the more they saw the misery of the present, the more they longed for the days of the past.

Germans had a deadly habit of seeking powerful leaders, leaders whom they would follow blindly. Frederick the Great, arguably Germany's finest leader, was nauseated by this servile tendency. His last attributed words on his deathbed were: "I am tired of ruling over slaves."

During postwar reconstruction Germany needed democratic leaders who would do better than the military dictators like Ludendorff who had gotten them into this world of depression and panic. The country was at a crossroads and needed a leader to take it forward to better days. And at this time, Germany had three possible contenders for leadership. First, there was General Hindenburg, who was not held responsible for the defeats over which he had presided and was still wildly popular.

Second, there was Ludendorff, who was not as popular, but who was acknowledged as the number two man and respected by conservatives for being a believer in law and order and a superb tactician. In many ways he was the darling of the multimillionaires, the plutocrats, the captains of industry, and the right-wing journalists because his ideas exonerated all of them from any wrongdoing at any time in the war, and because he glibly claimed Jews did the damage. Unfortunately for him, he was despised by the Left and by the intelligentsia, who saw his tales of conspiracy and his criticisms of the Socialists and Communists to be worse than dangerous, indeed to be utterly murderous.

And third, there was the powerful industrialist Walter Rathenau, the man who could talk sanely about Germany's prospects without degenerating into scapegoating and paranoia, the one major personage who was respected beyond Germany, especially in Britain.

Rathenau is a compelling case of what might-have-been. He had enormous abilities. Not only was he an educated engineer, he had also become an able politician. He had experience all over the globe. He had holdings overseas and twenty-one business endeavors around the world. He had the heart of a philanthropist. Thomas Edison, America's top inventor, had visited him and found him superior to all other Germans. "He knows things you have no idea of," said Edison. "This chap will one day accomplish, and know, more than all of us. This is a marvelous person."

Rathenau organized the mobilization of raw materials for the war and kept Germany going when it should have otherwise collapsed. He was, all in all, a living repudiation of the myth that the Jews had stabbed Germany in the back. But Ludendorff, author of the Stab in the Back legend, moved against him with full force.

Ludendorff's first days after the war started with a blast of self-pity. He mulled over his defeats and decided everyone was to blame but himself. Sometimes he blamed the Socialists and sometimes the anarchists, sometimes the strikers and sometimes the shirkers, sometimes the Kaiser and sometimes the government, sometimes the Vatican and sometimes the Masons, and always, always, he blamed the Jews.

Ludendorff expected to be judged in Prime Minister Lloyd George's threatened war crime trials. To avoid this, he abandoned his weary wife and fled cravenly to Sweden, where he went into hiding. There he continually muttered that he needed to "salvage the honor of the Fatherland, the Army, and my own Honor and Name."

Before, he despised the German soldiers who left their families and their nation and fled to foreign soil. Now he was doing what he had condemned, to be safe. But in exile he did not feel safe; he felt tortured. Leftists in Germany were threatening him from afar. And the many leftists in Sweden were doing the same. Many Swedes wanted him thrown out of the country, and the more zealous wanted him dead. Ludendorff scanned the map and suspected that only Finland might accept him. The Finns were grateful that he had sent troops and a naval squadron to quash a Communist revolt at the time of Brest-Litovsk, and he would probably have been welcome there at least under the present government. But that might change with time. Eventually, he knew, he might become stateless. It was at this time that he wrote a poignant letter to his long-suffering wife. "My heart was torn at leaving, and I miss you so," he wrote, uncharacteristically warm and sentimental. "To me it all seems like a bad dream. I do not know if I were right to go away. Things cannot go on like this forever. I say forever, but the whole thing has only just begun. . . . For four years I have fought for my country and now when so much is hanging in the balance, I must stand aside. I am at war with myself and the world. Dear, it is not easy to pull myself together again. . . . My nerves are so on edge and at times my speech loses control. There is no remedy. I feel my nerves have simply gone to pieces. . . Tell everyone that my fate is like Hannibal's [that is, thrown into exile after defeat and then forced to take poison]. That will help them understand what is happening to me. Keep these letters, dear. In the future they will form my memoirs."

Ludendorff did send more letters, and his wife received them, but she also received threats. People of the Left wanted her held hostage to force Ludendorff to return for trial. Ludendorff may have been the only person in the war whom his enemies and his own countrymen both wanted to hang. Soon there were angry people demonstrating outside her window. The neighbors wanted her thrown into the street.

It seemed Ludendorff and his family were unable to escape his past. Soon the Liberal Party in Sweden was demanding that the government expel him. It was wretched, and he felt like a boxer hit hard. But however unsteady he felt, Ludendorff was magnificent in one remarkable sense. Whatever his faults, he managed to focus, and he began to write his memoirs. Here he defended every aspect of the war from his own perspective. And not surprisingly he attributed all missteps to others. Within three months his memoirs were finished.

Then, in February 1919 Ludendorff learned from sources inside Germany that among the conservatives, he still had friends and supporters who liked his Stab in the Back story, and they told him that he could return safely if he wished. This surprised him. There had been a movement in Germany to put him on trial, but there were also several powerful members of the elite classes who had only respect for his tales of how the Jews had ruined the nation. And these elites let him know that he would be welcomed back to the land he had ruined. They wanted him as a symbol, to whitewash their record.

The Junker types were especially pleased with Ludendorff because they sensed that he was ultimately an arch-conservative like themselves and, even more importantly, because his Stab in the

Back legend managed to deflect all blame away from their class and to deliver it forcefully upon this Jewish conspiracy, which was said to have done such terrible harm.

So Ludendorff returned and was astonished to be given a posh suite at the Adlon Hotel, the best in Berlin, opposite the Brandenburg Gate, where he signed the register as "Herr Neumann." This meant "new man"—clearly Ludendorff saw himself as a new person, one who would start the struggle again. The Adlon managers encouraged him in this messianic spirit and deferred to him most cravenly. They let him use a private exit onto the street so that he could avoid the high-ranking Allied officers also staying there. He would not have to look his conqueror in the face.

Relieved, he worked his memoirs through a last revision, and in July 1919 he got them published. One of his erstwhile assistants, Max Hoffmann, a superlative general with a reputation for integrity, declared the memoirs worthless, indeed dangerous. The accomplished military historian Hans Delbrück of the University of Berlin agreed. Delbrück was the author of a four-volume history of war and a former member of the Reichstag, and therefore was an expert judge of the recent past, both military and political. And he tore the memoirs apart page by page and warned the public that the criminals who had ruined Germany were two famous frauds, Ludendorff and Hindenburg, and not any mysterious cabal of Jews at the home front. Said he: "One simply pulls out one's hair when one reads such thoughts. Every sentence is either an absurdity or a lie."

Hoffmann was right that as a historical document, the memoirs were unreliable. And Delbruck was right that they were absurd. Yet they did serve a purpose. Years later English writer Samuel Hynes noted that the Ludendorff memoir was a "self-monument" to demonstrate the greatness of his being. The average German, who knew nothing of the inside history of the conflict, was fooled into believing that Ludendorff was a man of greatness, sabotaged only by swinish Jews. Over and over the memoirs told the same tale: The good character of the German Army and the nation was always maintained. Only the leftist politicians and the Jews were dishonorable. No German need blush while looking at the record of the military in this conflict. And of course Ludendorff's glowing reputation was held up as perfect.

With the memoirs published, Ludendorff ensured that his stab-in-the-back legend became gospel truth. It could go on for decades. And if people believed the legend were true, then they would believe the new Weimar Republic was false. Therefore the republic and the Jews deserved to die. William L. Shirer, in his monumental 900-page work *Rise and Fall of the Third Reich*, a firsthand report on Germany from 1919 to 1945, spoke to this when he declared that "the legend of the Stab in the Back, more than anything else, would undermine the Weimar Republic and pave the way for Hitler's ultimate triumph."

This legend did wonders for Ludendorff. Ultimately it convinced millions of Germans that they were never defeated in the disastrous Ludendorff Offensives, which meant that his suicidal strategies were noble. By 1924 he was able to coax the learned editors of the *Encyclopedia Britannica* to print a powerful essay of his myths under the title "Germany, Never Defeated!" which the trusting editors foolishly presented at face value, not yet aware that they were publishing lies that would someday lead to the murder of millions.

The document should not have been published by this fine source, for its lies were legion. In it, Ludendorff made clear that in 1918 he was winning his world war until, one terrible day in August, he and his army were ruined by "internal disruption" in the German government, caused by "revolutionary agitation." All adverse ideas and defeatism, he said, were caused by "enemy propaganda." Most amazingly, he then declared piously that if he had been left to his own devices, he wanted to make a peace "without annexations or indemnities," which was exactly the peace he would not give the Russians at Brest.

So it was that Ludendorff convinced Germany that its punitive treaty with the Allies was dishonorable and that it was therefore not binding. So Germans came to believe that the nation's friends were men like Ludendorff, the heroes of Germany, when indeed these men were the gravediggers, who would soon ravage Germany for a second time.

Consequently, Jews became enemies for betraying these heroes. This story was told and retold, with great embellishments. And the final versions meant something deadly that few understood at the time. They meant that the inclination to butcher the Jews to punish them for their crimes was an idiocy of Ludendorff's that started in 1919, long before Hitler. Tragically, Ludendorff's savageries had a logic. To put the Holocaust, or Sho'ah, in one murderous phrase: Because Jews had sabotaged Germany, Germany had to kill them in justifiable revenge.

This required a massive rewriting of history. Cleverly, Ludendorff flipped several sequences to blame the Jews. The truth of what happened in 1918, before Ludendorff rewrote it, was simple. In 1918, Ludendorff lost the war with the Ludendorff Offensives, and *then* there were massive strikes that paralyzed the nation. Unable to advance and unable to win, Ludendorff begged for the politicians to make peace, then made the politicians take deadly responsibility for making that peace.

To the delight of the German generals, the Pan-German League, the plutocrats, and the extreme right, Ludendorff cleverly reversed this sequence. In his telling, Germany was winning, but traitors broke out a rash of strikes that paralyzed the army, cut off the munitions, and led to defeat. These criminals then sued cravenly for peace, in an act of pure treason, when they could have had a splendid German victory.

No one asked who the criminals were in this conspiracy or why they did this. The conspiracy story made no sense, but the far right heard it and said it so often that everyone believed it. Hitler wrote of this conspiracy in chapter 7 of *Mein Kampf* when describing the debacle of 1918: "When out of the cool nights the Allied soldiers already seemed to hear the dull rumble of the advancing storm units of the German Army, and with eyes fixed in fear and trembling awaited the approaching judgment, suddenly a flaming red light rose in Germany, casting its glow into the last shell holes of the enemy front. At the very moment when the German divisions were receiving their last instructions for the great attack, the General Strike broke out in all of its armaments factories, thus depriving the German Army of crucial arms and ammunition."

Hitler also wrote of a workers' strike at this time: "It strengthened the enemy belief in victory and relieved the paralyzing despair of the Allied front. In the time that followed, thousands of German soldiers had to pay for this with their blood. The instigators of this vilest mass of scoundrel tricks were Jews, and unions led by Jews."

As Ludendorff knew better than any other man in Germany, the truth was the opposite. Nearly all the strikes of 1918 came after

Ludendorff failed and his soldiers retreated. To say that these events were a cause of the German defeat was a lie. They were the result.

The leaders of the Weimar Republic failed to inform public opinion. Anyone reading the history texts they allowed in the German schools over the next years would be staggered to see how World War I was treated. Spencer C. Tucker wrote a major work titled *The European Powers in the First World War,* in which he rued: "Not a single school textbook of the interwar period would show the role played by General Erich Ludendorff or the General Staff in Germany's collapse." Instead, "people found comfort in a simple explanation for German defeat and postwar troubles." Jeffrey Verhey, in his solid study published by Cambridge University Press, *The Spirit of 1914,* explains clearly that "during the 1920s it was almost impossible to find a nationalistic narrative of the War that did not include the Stab in the Back legend."

At this time Walter Rathenau, though a Jew, had risen to the position of minister of foreign affairs. He was the only Jew in the nation at a cabinet-level position, hardly an indication that Jews had overwhelming influence. And far from conspiring behind the scenes, he was openly doing everything possible to stabilize the economy.

He had a great mind, and he might have been able to turn everything around. He was one of the most successful and patriotic industrialists in Germany. Rathenau was admired by most foreign observers and was the hope of progressives, in Germany and beyond. English writer Robert Boothby wrote of Rathenau: "He was . . . a prophet, a philosopher, a mystic, a writer, a statesman, an industrial magnate of the highest and greatest order, and the pioneer of . . . industrial rationalization." If anyone could save Germany, it was Rathenau.

And now Rathenau was coming out with statements that Germany *could* pay the reparations that the Allies demanded. Later the American economist Bernard Baruch said the same. One of the founders of the German Democratic Party, Rathenau was full of ideas for a better Germany, but he was slowly being surrounded by thugs with long knives.

Soon he was receiving threats every day, and these continued for months. In the streets men chanted, "Kill Walter Rathenau, the goddamn German Jew!" And then Ludendorff moved in for the kill. He made statements linking Rathenau to the Jewish conspiracy that had ruined the fatherland. Ludendorff published his book *Warfare and Politics* in Berlin in 1922, and in this powerful 372-page diatribe, he slandered Rathenau as one of the topmost Jews who had killed the boys in the trenches. He also declared Rathenau to be one of the Elders of Zion, the devilish conspirators who were said to meet every year in secret, in a fabled cemetery in Switzerland, to plot the downfall of Christians everywhere. No matter that *The Protocols of the Learned Elders of Zion* was a clumsy forgery done in 1905 by a lunatic Russian monk who was disowned even by the czar of Russia. No matter that the *London Times* had proven the work a fraud in 1920, with the able help of the famed writers of the Graves family. This did not stop Ludendorff. A widely admired German historian named Wolfram Wette recently has shown how far Ludendorff took this. In his study on the German defense forces, *The Wehrmacht: History, Myth, Reality*, published by Harvard University Press in 2009, Wette writes: "Ludendorff, a pronounced anti-Semite, attempted to forge a link between Rathenau and the legend of the Stab in the Back. His defamatory statements would have far-reaching effect, and several scholars regard Ludendorff as largely responsible for Rathenau's later assassination."

Ludendorff told endless tales linking Rathenau to Communist conspiracies. One of them is still believed today: Ludendorff alleged that Rathenau's younger sister, Edith, married the fiery Jewish Communist Karl Radek, who had accompanied Lenin to Russia years before and had written the brainy propaganda that Lenin then used against the Germans. This was untrue—Edith had married a banker named Andreae, but Ludendorff repeated the Radek connection so often that it acquired a life of its own. Even today in 2016, the marriage of Edith Rathenau and Karl Radek is reported as fact in the *Britannica Concise Encyclopedia* and other solid sources.

Ludendorff also knew that Rathenau, as minister of foreign affairs, had recently signed a modest cooperation treaty with Russia, the Treaty of Rapallo, which normalized relations between Russia and Germany. This normalization process had required that the two nations dissolve the ferocious Treaty of Brest-Litovsk, that brutal document that no one could enforce in the first place and that theoretically gave Germany a fourth of Russia. The treaty's arrogance and impossibility were such that Ludendorff should have been ashamed of it. But Ludendorff was proud of his herculean work in negotiating this treaty. He saw it as an achievement. The dissolution of this treaty probably antagonized him. And the fact that a Jew dissolved it might have made it worse for Ludendorff, for whom hating Jews was now becoming a way of life.

Cleverly, Ludendorff blended these lies so that Rathenau was soon seen to be leading a Jewish plot against the fatherland and to have family relations in the Russian government who would be happy to overwhelm Germany.

This conspiracy reached its zenith one June morning in 1922. As Rathenau's open limousine took him toward the Foreign Ministry, it was overtaken by a Mercedes touring car in which sat two navy personnel. One tossed a grenade into Rathenau's limousine while the other shot him with an MP-18 submachine gun. The blast and bullets shredded his legs, while blood gushed from his mouth. A nurse who was walking nearby rushed to help, but Rathenau could not speak. He stared, mouthed words, and then went still. In seconds he was gone.

Thus Ludendorff and his kind helped murder the one man who could have saved Germany. He could have engineered a rational peace and kept the nation away from World War II. He could have paid the reparations, or at least much of them. And he could have protected the Jews.

There was an investigation, which should have uncovered something, but the authorities were lethargic. They rounded up the usual suspects and did identify the second tier of ringleaders, but they punished only the lower echelons. And of the three men convicted, no one was executed. When a couple of the killers eventually died years after, the Nazis turned their graves into shrines, with statues and flowers and military band performances.

The thugs with long knives then came closer. Rathenau's sister Edith was threatened. Although the best writers in the nation loved her salon, the Villa Andreae, and said that she was the top intellectual woman in Berlin, she feared for her life. Men like Hermann Hesse and Thomas Mann swore by her, but so many wanted her dead that she left for Switzerland, where she and her husband lived the rest of their lives.

Anti-Semitism was rising, as was Ludendorff's prestige. Indeed the two were related.

The police investigation of the murderers revealed that the killers hoped the death of Rathenau would unleash a civil war, which in turn would cause the right to take power and put Ludendorff in office, because he was seen as the best person to punish Jews for their crimes. The stab-in-the-back tale was doing wonders for Ludendorff's reputation and power.

Liberals who were anything like Rathenau were living on borrowed time in the new Germany. Indeed, the writer Franz Kafka found it incredible that Rathenau lived as long as he did. And the London *Spectator* editorialized that this great man's death was as predictable as tomorrow's sunrise. The prime minister of Britain went further and called it "national suicide." He understood what Rathenau could have done to save Germany, as well as what would happen to Germany without the influence of this peaceful genius.

Several other important pacifist heroes died during this time. Matthias Erzberger, the unlucky man who signed the armistice and tried in vain to tell Germans that this treaty was negotiated at Ludendorff's insistence, was murdered by former soldiers on a quiet afternoon in the Black Forest. The Socialist Karl Liebknecht was dragged out of his car and shot in the back. Fiery Rosa Luxemburg, a Socialist thinker, was tortured and shot, then thrown into a river. The pacifist Hans Paasche, who helped persecuted people leave Germany, was shot when his home in the country was attacked by sixty soldiers pretending they were looking for dangerous weapons. And there were others, too many others.

Kurt Tucholsky, a German-Jewish journalist and critic of Ludendorff who had served in the war, described how militarists like Ludendorff functioned. First they slaughtered millions of their men in the trenches. Second, after they lost the war, they killed the critics in the cities. Third, they rendered the assassins immune from justice. Fourth, they went out to find new victims. This sequence, when repeated enough, Tucholsky said, rendered Germany unfit for living. As he put it in December 1922, after an inept investigation into the death of Rathenau ended inconclusively: "The German political murder of the past years is schematic and systematic. . . . Everything is certain from the outset: The incentives from organized backers; the murder by ambush; the sloppy investigation; the lazy excuses; the few weak phrases; then the lenient punishments, plus suspended sentences. This is not bad justice, this is not poor justice, this is no justice."

Tucholsky left Germany and never returned. It was not a good time for original thinkers.

But it was a good time for conspirators. Ludendorff began to get a wider following. Slowly he began to construct what has been called "the Ludendorff Circle," a cluster of interconnected supporters who helped him. The group involved various personnel, not too closely organized but highly influential all the same. It included military groups, paramilitary organizations, right-wing journalists, and even a few monarchists. Together this ramshackle coalition gave Ludendorff enough support to make him, for a time, the prime critic of the Weimar Republic. The members of this circle were remarkably consistent in one regard: They all worked together to destroy the government.

Ludendorff published tracts and books with the most arresting titles: *The Nation at War*, *Ludendorff's Own Story*, *Total War*, *The Next War*. Some sold badly; some sold well. *The Next War*, a book about how the next war should be a total war and should be fought ruthlessly, with Jews jailed or butchered, sold handsomely.

The message was the same in his postwar works, and the catch-phrases were endlessly repeated. Ludendorff's doctrine, in para-phrase, was as follows:

War is the natural state of man, which brings out the best in a people. War is without end and is the magnificent contest for which Germany is better qualified than all others. Peace is the bothersome interval between your last war and the next. It is neither desirable nor manly. We Germans used to say that war is the continuation of politics by other means. That has changed. We live in a new age where politics are subordinated to war. Warriors are in charge in this new world. Politicians are there to serve them. Modern life de-mands a military leader, and the politicians should wait upon him.

It was as if Ludendorff were declaring the words attributed to Louis XIV, "I am the state."

Ludendorff preached that this new kind of war demanded an in-creased commitment, with the people at the home front integrated into the conflict as never before. It demanded an improvement of Germany's people and their stock, their thinking, and their living. They had to be pure, turn inward, and embrace the old Germanic gods. Ludendorff preached that Christianity was an inferior reli-gion for the weak and far too Jewish. As he put it chillingly: "Are you a German or are you a Christian?"

Through the 1920s and 1930s Ludendorff joined various and sundry conspiracies. In March 1920, he supported a right-wing journalist named Wolfgang Kapp, who had been born in New York City but had visited Ludendorff in Sweden during his exile there. Ludendorff and Kapp had come to some kind of understanding, and Kapp then moved to Germany. There he actually seized Berlin with some disaffected soldiers, and for forty-eight hours he managed to chase the government out of town, to Dresden. For a moment Kapp and his thugs had a chance of success, and they declared that they chose Ludendorff to be a dictator, to save the nation.

But poor Kapp, who signed himself "Chancellor of the Reich," could not get important supporters to follow him. The Kapp ministers turned out to be desperate characters, and the public failed to become interested in a government by gangsters.

The Weimar Republic had no soldiers it could trust to put down the coup because the men at the top were cautiously sympathetic. The commander of the German Navy, Admiral Adolf von Trotha, also seemed close to coming out in favor of the coup. In Bavaria, right-wing fanatics were in sympathy, and politician Gustav Ritter von Kahr was said to be about to declare himself in favor. For a moment it looked like the extreme right might support the coup and Ludendorff might be returned to power.

But the workers of Berlin were magnificent, and they called a general strike that spread over Germany like fire. Ten million refused to work, bringing the nation to its knees. By March 17, Kapp and his goons had discovered that the generals in the army were now against them. Kapp had no significant support except Ludendorff.

And Ludendorff was not enough.

Kapp and his thugs fled by car, his coup a farce. Ludendorff should have been tried for treason, but because of his prestige from World War I, the government spared him. So he retreated to his villa outside Munich and wandered in his garden, walking among his statues of the old German gods and talking to himself.

Then, in the autumn of 1923, Ludendorff joined an abler thug named Hitler for a coup in Munich, the so-called Ludendorff–Hitler Putsch. This was the most serious of Ludendorff's efforts to regain power. Special pins were wrought with the slogan "Heil Hitler–Ludendorff!," which the faithful wore on their lapels. One such pin is pictured on the cover of this book. With several hundred of their newly trained storm troopers, Hitler and Ludendorff tried to spark a revolution.

Although it failed, this farce had serious overtones. On the night of November 23, 1923, Hitler and nineteen newly minted Nazis, at the head of several hundred soldiers, advanced to a huge beer hall in downtown Munich. Hitler had Ludendorff walk beside him in the uniform of a field marshal. The two were accompanied by Rudolf Hess, Ernst Röhm, and Hermann Göring. Dramatically, Hitler fired his pistol into the ceiling of the beer hall and shouted: "The national revolution has broken out! This hall is filled with 600 men! Nobody is allowed to leave!"

Hitler declared that they were deposing the government and were forming a new administration with Ludendorff as its head. He asked the men not to be afraid. He said his revolution was only against the Jews and the "November Criminals" who had signed the traitorous peace in November 1918 with the Allied Powers. The hypocrisy of Ludendorff's being here is breathtaking, as he was one of the top persons in Germany to demand that they sign the treaty in the first place. All in all he was pretending to go after criminals . . . like himself!

Then Hitler declared that he and Ludendorff were committed to saving the country at this desperate eleventh hour. He said, "One last thing I can tell you, either the German Revolution begins tonight, or we will be dead by dawn."

Ludendorff then shouted, "We will march!" and tried to lead a contingent toward the Bavarian Defense Ministry. But the state police stopped them cold, and Ludendorff's glorious march lasted one minute.

The police counterattacked, killing sixteen Nazis and wounding others. Hitler was wounded and arrested, as were his cohorts. Hermann Göring, the aviation expert, was shot in the groin and given massive doses of morphine. The morphine would become a habit and would corrupt his mind so thoroughly that in the next war, he would be the general most responsible for losing Dunkirk and Stalingrad.

Eventually the German state put these Nazis on trial, but the trial was a travesty. The judge openly said how much he admired Hitler. And for the twenty-four days of the trial, the young Hitler was able to rave about saving Germany from everything—from Jews, Communists, Socialists, Masons . . . whomever. As for his famous accomplice, Ludendorff, the judge allowed the defense to pretend that he just happened to be in the neighborhood—in a field marshal's uniform!—when the coup broke out, so he was then allowed to claim that he had not been involved. Hitler should have been shot for treason, but the judge merely gave him nine months in prison.

This crisis gave Hitler legitimacy, allowing him to be seen standing next to Ludendorff as an equal and to make grand speeches in court to the applause of the judges and the fanatics in the galleries. Also, the time in prison gave Hitler the opportunity to write his memoir, *Mein Kampf*, which became an instant best seller.

Hitler's next move was masterful. In the 1925 elections for the presidency of Germany, he convinced Ludendorff to run as a coalition candidate for the new Nazi Party, and he was glad to have this famous, raving man pushing his scapegoat concepts against the Jews. Hitler expected Ludendorff to lose, but he knew that this association with Ludendorff would give Nazis the national exposure they needed to be taken seriously. National Socialism was then an obscure and barely noticed cult. With Ludendorff as their candidate in this coalition, they would be seen as a significant movement endorsed by one of the two most important German generals of the war.

Ludendorff ran against his old master Hindenburg, who was much more popular, and Ludendorff antagonized many of his fellow soldiers by his virulent statements against the old general. To add farce to tragedy, Ludendorff also came out in favor of prohibition, which in a beer-drinking nation like Germany was a rotten plank to add to any political platform.

Consequently, Ludendorff received just 1 percent of the vote. His superior, Hindenburg, got 48 percent and won the election. Ludendorff's showing was abysmal, given his fame in the world war. But although Ludendorff lost, Hitler was content. He had won a legitimacy that he needed, and he was able to proceed with confidence.

This loss at the ballot box seems to have unbalanced Ludendorff. Historians have trouble evaluating this with certainty, but many scholars, like Professor Roger Chickering of Georgetown University, have said that sometime in the 1920s, Ludendorff became especially unglued.

Whatever his state of mind, Ludendorff was getting into criminal schemes that were lunatic. He soon got involved in a plot to make counterfeit money. First he linked up with a pack of criminal

Hungarians who wanted to print French money and pass it in the Netherlands. The group included a Hungarian prince named Lajos Windisgraetz and the chaplain to the Hungarian Army, Bishop Istvan Zadravetz, and together with Ludendorff they proceeded with their plan. They acquired 4.5 tons of special paper and printed 30,000,000 French francs. The printing was perfect, the ink was right, but a banker in the Netherlands felt that the paper was wrong and called the police. Ludendorff's career as a counterfeiter had lasted one day.

Ludendorff then got mixed up in fortune telling. According to his mystical predictions, in 1932 there would be a war in which France, Italy, and Russia would attack Germany. Soon after he made this prediction, he warned that the pope was engaged in hostile acts against the fatherland and advised anyone who would listen that patriots should fight the Vatican. He was convinced that Hitler was not extreme enough against conspiracies, especially those of the pope, and soon went on a crusade against that Nazi too. He composed a pamphlet with the farfetched title *Hitler's Betrayal of the German People to the Roman Pope*.

Ludendorff's ferocious tirades and schemes during these years devastated his wife, Margarethe. She had been melancholic since the war and the loss of her beloved sons. And, as she wrote in a memoir, "Among Ludendorff's regular visitors was a distinguished looking lady in deep mourning. She came every day. . . . She told me that it was urgently necessary . . . to know Ludendorff's whereabouts in order to keep in touch with him. . . . She produced a bulky envelope and extracted from me a promise to forward it to him. . . . She often came afterwards with the same request, to which I conscientiously acceded."

Later Margarethe discovered that the envelope contained love letters: "The correspondence had not the remotest connection with politics, but consisted, to cut a long story short, of love letters to Ludendorff. The lady had employed me, his lawful wife, as the postmistress for her intrigue. . . . The whole business revealed her as fundamentally lacking in any sense of decency."

The loss of her sons and the loss of her husband's love, together, were too much for this refined woman, and she went into decline. Ludendorff took advantage of her state and locked her up in an asylum, where the doctors drugged her into a stupor to keep her silent. They had need. The last thing Ludendorff wanted was for his wife to tell the world how his tales of conspiracy were lies. Ludendorff then offered a cover story that explained how she had always been a morphine addict and thus made her appear wholly unreliable. He then divorced her ruthlessly, kept her locked up, and married the mysterious woman who had sent him the passionate love letters—a psychiatrist in the Völkisch movement named Mathilde von Kemnitz.

Mathilde von Kemnitz may be the most eccentric character in this book. William Sheridan Allen, in his book *The Infancy of Nazism*, noted that Mathilde began her career by seducing a rich youth named Gustav von Kremnitz. She married him and had children with him, but then his parents annulled the union and disowned the "bastards," as they called them. Undeterred, she abandoned the children and went off to marry Major Edward Georg Kline, who then died in mysterious circumstances. Did she murder him? No one knows. She then met Adolf Hitler and tried to be intimate with him, but Hitler was briefed by his intelligence officers and obtained not only information about her terrible past but also nude photos from her youthful days.

For several reasons Hitler did not find her enticing. Mathilde pretended to be a scholar, claiming to have a PhD with top honors in neurology, which she did not have. Some top-ranking Nazis described her as being like an onion. If you peeled off the layers—the layer that was a woman, the layer that was a scholar, the layer that was a priestess, the layer that was a patriot—you had left only a stinking onion.

Like Ludendorff, Mathilde became a strong critic of the Christian religions. She was convinced that Christian priests had murdered 9,000,000 magical Aryan witches in the past and that she, a good witch, had to defend herself. To obtain this estimate, Mathilde studied a twenty-year period when witches were persecuted in Europe, and she calculated that if the same percentage of witches had been attacked over the previous eighteen centuries in every major nation, then 9,000,000 women had been burned at the stake. This idea, which eventually influenced Nazi dogma, was quaint. As Michael D. Bailey of Iowa State University has noted in his book *Magic and Superstition in Europe*, Mathilde claimed to have discovered a Christian conspiracy to destroy Aryan women so that Aryans would disappear from the earth. Mathilde wrote a pamphlet titled *Christian Cruelty to German Women,* in which she branded Christianity a Jewish plot, with a nasty Jew named Jesus who was bent on killing Aryans. Above all she despised the way this Jewish conspiracy taught meekness, which she said was the Jews' way to cripple the stronger races.

She was also convinced that Jews were swine who were dominated by the Dalai Lama of Tibet. Through the 1920s and '30s, she would warn how "this priestly class" at "the Top of the World," the Tibetans, were effecting a "mental invasion" of Europe and that Aryan Germans were at risk.

After failing to seduce Hitler, Mathilde got to know Ludendorff, and she pursued the general, who was still important. And here she was lucky, for Ludendorff became her ticket to fame and her meal ticket. She got close to him and was able to echo his fears and premonitions, and she was also able to make a mental catalogue of his ideas. In the most exalted manner, she convinced him that through him Germany would be reborn. She told Ludendorff that he would lead the new Germany to glory. She convinced him that he was destined to go through a process of self-creation and that she would help him discover the natural gods of Germany, who would guide him on this long, mystical voyage.

Mathilde strove to make a pure Germanic philosophy composed of Nietzsche, Kant, and Schopenhauer. She especially embraced Nietzsche's belief that the Superman is above the law, in the same way that Ludendorff saw himself as above the law. Nietzsche's Übermensch, or Superman, is the creature who would emerge when a man with great potential mastered himself, shook off Christianity's "herd mentality," and created his own superior values.

Mathilde and Erich Ludendorff pieced together a pastiche of Nietzschean philosophy in which the new German man was to become godlike in his views and powers. He would be a Superman by being all-pure—that is, by being uncontaminated by foreigners, Jews, Masons, and Christians. Mathilde saw a glorious German nation under Ludendorff. This was the rock of her new world.

Her codification of Ludendorff's ideas was ramshackle. and in some respects it was only a jumbled conglomeration, but the process calmed Ludendorff for the first time in years. As Ludendorff put it: "My acquaintance with the earliest work of Doctor Mathilde Kemnitz was of decisive influence on the course of my inner struggle."

Ludendorff explained his realization this way: "Gradually I recognized the pernicious forces which had caused the collapse of the [German] people [in World War I] and in them the real enemies of the freedom of the German Race. . . . I became aware of the fungi within the structure of our society . . . in the form of secret supranational forces, i.e., the Jewish people and Rome, along with their tools, the Freemasons, the Jesuit order, and the occult and satanic formations."

Mathlide taught Ludendorff that real Germans should avoid Christian compassion and never help the weak. She took Ludendorff by the hand and led him back to the garden at their home in Tutzing, near Munich, where they stood surrounded by their statues of the German gods. Here the two felt comfort in their dreams about a new German religion, of which they would be the prophets.

"Man requires and needs something which he can obey unquestioningly," said Ludendorff. Ludendorff saw himself giving the orders, of course, because he was the Superman destined to reenter the corridors of power. And he saw the masses of Germans as his future loyal supporters. It was just a matter of time, Ludendorff felt, and the country would call him. And he saw himself as the military leader of the new Germany when the country was ready to go to war again.

Together the Ludendorffs tried to get people to take them seriously. At one time they owned several bookstores and a publishing house called Ludendorff Verlag, and they gave talks to large audiences. Estimates indicate that they had a following of about 100,000 readers, plus another 30,000 soldiers in a nostalgic association they called the Tannenberg League.

Interestingly, Mathilde was much like Princess Hermione of Schoenaich-Carolath, now married to ex-Kaiser Wilhelm II.

Hermine also whispered to her husband that he would come back to power and restore Germany's glories. She invited top Nazi officials, like the rotund Hermann Göring, Hitler's new morphine-addicted minister, to dinner. She treated Göring like visiting royalty. She gave him money and proposed toasts. "To the coming Reich!" she would cheer.

"To the coming Kaiser," Göring would return.

The idea of these people returning to power was not a complete fantasy. The Kaiser, Ludendorff, and Hitler were all rather alike. They all believed in *The Protocols of the Elders of Zion,* they all endorsed the tales of Jewish conspiracy, and they believed the stab-in-the-back legend. They also upheld its ancillary concept, that Germany needed to not only bash the Jews but also to launch a world war to avenge the past. These people saw the Nazis as the "wave of the future," as some called them. Indeed, the term was coined to describe the Nazis in the first place. These people fit into the zeitgeist of the time and had every possibility of taking power.

By this time in the 1930s, many Germans were careening toward the same frightening goals. Many believed that humankind had not reached its potential. Ludendorff and Hitler both believed that the Germanic Superman would master his emotions and elevate his instincts to create a higher kind of human. This would produce a master race, which would lead the world. And their examples of the ideal Supermen were . . . themselves!

One way or another, Germany was unbalanced between 1914 and 1945, and a case could be made that World Wars I and II were an insane continuum that started with the slow rise of Ludendorff as de facto dictator by 1916 and ended with the suicide of Hitler in his pathetic bunker in 1945.

Ludendorff in the 1930s soon became problematic, however, because fewer and fewer were listening to him. Power was shifting to Hitler, who, despite his huge weaknesses, was a masterful propagandist and far more interesting to the masses. At this time Ludendorff had at best some 100,000 followers and his power base was shrinking. He became angry, and he picked fights with his old allies. He feuded with Hindenburg; fought with Rupprecht, crown prince of Bavaria, to the point of a lawsuit; and clashed with Admiral von Tirpitz, who used to be a friend. The poet Kurt Tucholsky, a veteran of the Great War who despised all these men as degenerate militarists, scorned Ludendorff in a ditty that was widely circulated:

> Are you anxious, Erich, Are you frightened, Erich?
> Does your heart pound, Erich? Are you running away?
> Do the Masons, Erich, and the Jesuits, Erich,
> Do they want to knife you, Erich? What a fright!
> These Jews are becoming more and more unattractive.
> These Jews are creating all our misfortunes!

Ludendorff even began to feud with his onetime friend Hitler. When Hitler came to visit, after he ascended to power, he offered Ludendorff the rank of field marshal, but the old general disliked "this little corporal," as he called him, and thundered back, "Field marshals are born, not made!"

These two men had much in common; they should have gotten along. But truth to tell, neither man could subordinate himself to the other. And neither could share power with anyone. Further, Hitler could not stand Ludendorff's wife, as he knew about her tainted past.

So in the end Ludendorff was left alone with his dreams and his bizarre wife. His final tracts of philosophy were so zany that they defy analysis. One month he was writing a tract that said that Jews had killed Schubert. Next he declared that Jews had killed Mozart. Next he accused them of killing Friedrich Schiller. Then in all seriousness he accused them of killing Marie Antoinette.

On March 31, 1937, the *Manchester Guardian* of England reported that Ludendorff was still esteemed in a few Nazi circles and would possibly be called to head the German Army. The *New York Post* was skeptical and noted: "Ludendorff is, to put it mildly, an odd character." The paper said that he added considerably to "the Mad Hatter atmosphere that clings to the Third Reich."

Possibly Ludendorff could have returned to power in some way. Hitler always said that he was grateful to Ludendorff for his support in the 1920s, when Ludendorff made the Nazis respectable. The madness of Ludendorff was hardly an issue, because Hitler's inner circle was replete with psychopaths, lunatics, and pure fools. Indeed, in Hitler's cabinet there was perhaps only one relatively sane person, the architect Albert Speer, and even he was a mass murderer.

But Ludendorff could not live without Mathilde, and Hitler could not abide her, so eventually the Nazis ignored Ludendorff, and Hitler even ordered that the presses of Germany could no longer print his writings.

In the end Ludendorff had only a few followers. Miserable and despising the world, he died in his sleep from a diseased liver on December 20, 1937, at a hospital near Munich. Cynics quipped that many other parts of him were diseased too, especially his brain. Ironically, he died in a Catholic hospital and he was tended by gentle nuns during his last hours. One hopes that he did not lecture them on how the pope was out to destroy Germany.

Hitler, though hardly on good terms with Ludendorff, gave instructions for a fine state funeral. To glorify the dead Ludendorff was to glorify the Nazi Party, and for this the German Army came out in force with military bands and solemn processions. SS soldiers carried his medals on velvet cushions as they moved his body on a gigantic bier, pulled by black stallions, to the grave. It was a powerful spectacle.

The only surprising aspect of the funeral was that Ludendorff's coffin was covered with the obsolete battle flag of old Prussia, which was completely out of date. The swastika of Hitler's new Germany was nowhere to be seen. To a few observers, this suggested a parting of the ways, but most people did not notice. It was pathetic. The once-glorious general had no friends even among the Nazis he had helped to power.

At the funeral, the German Army band played a sentimental military song, "The Good Comrade," adapted from a poem written in 1809 in which a soldier sighs about the death of his best pal in the army:

> In battle he was my comrade.
> There was no better friend I had.
> The drum called us to battle,
> And he was always at my side,
> Marching in step with me.
> But a bullet came whistling toward us.
> Was it for him or was it for me?
> He fell in the dust,
> And I lost a part of me.

The song gave the impression that the soldiers had a friend in Ludendorff, a good fellow whom they would have loved. As it was played, the guard saluted.

Hitler came to the funeral with his storm troopers, and people expected him to speak as the coffin was lowered into the earth. A story was circulated that Hitler whispered, "Goodbye, son of Valhalla!" as it went down. But that, like many of the stories about Ludendorff, was untrue. Hitler said not a word. What Hitler might have said is hard to imagine. He and Ludendorff were alike in philosophy but they disliked one another. They were identical in their fanaticism, in their belief in the Germanic Superman, and in their demand that Germany win a new world war and eliminate the Jews. Yet they distrusted one another totally.

The American press was kind regarding the death of this man. On January 17, 1938, a multipage obituary in *Life* magazine praised Ludendorff as Germany's best general of the war and gave no hint of his lies and crimes. His extending World War I beyond 1916, his doubling of the casualties of that war, and his losing that war received no mention. The article also said that Ludendorff was equal to Robert E. Lee. This is like saying that Benedict Arnold was the equal of George Washington. And so one of the worst men in history was buried with honors.

Years later, in 1999, Steven T. Naftzger, a doctoral candidate from the City University of New York's History Department, visited the town of Tutzing in Bavaria, where Ludendorff was buried. He told his young German friends he was doing a study on Ludendorff, and they said they had not heard of him. But their fathers knew.

"Only fathers know such things," one said.

Then Naftzger went looking for the grave in the three different cemeteries in town. Eventually, off in the corner of the last of the cemeteries, he managed to find the site. There was a slender monument seven feet tall in bronze, with a sword and a weathered face of the man. It was overgrown with vines and the student saw no evidence that people visited the grave. No one tended the plot, no one left flowers, and no one cared.

Naftzger pried the vines off the plaque and was disappointed to see that it merely gave the man's name and birth and death dates. It offered no details of the man's life. This general, one of the major players of the century, the only general significant in both world wars, left not a trace behind.

There are no monuments to Ludendorff anywhere in Germany either. When that student went to Ludendorff's former home and knocked on the door, the current owner came out and conceded that he had a private monument inside, but he would not show it. Naftzger wrote: "It is odd that in less than two generations this man, who controlled the destiny of his country [and much of the world] . . . has become obscure."

Ludendorff had more power than any German since Frederick the Great, and he is nearly unknown. He was integral to killing 6,000,000 Jews, but he is now sidestepped by most historians. He lies forgotten in an obscure cemetery that no man visits.

Perhaps it is necessary for Germans to forget this man and what he did. They can dismiss Hitler as a madman from the fringe of society, not really Germanic, for whom they are not really responsible. But Ludendorff, who helped make Hitler possible, cannot be dismissed this way—indeed he cannot be dismissed at all. Ludendorff came from the uppermost level of German power and held rank second to none. He was the center of his government, and he was integral to the entire German experience of the First World War. He contributed definitively to the death of millions, the butchering of nations, the Russian Revolution, and two world wars. For a time, this man *was* Germany. And it may be uncomfortable for Germans to see that their countrymen, from the Kaiser on down, could accept his ideas and die for them.

When Ludendorff lost the First World War, the Germans gladly accepted his stab-in-the-back legend to explain the defeat. This legend served as the basis for destroying the Weimar Republic in the 1920s, for hurting the Jews in the 1930s, and for launching the new world war in the 1940s. Did any person do more harm in the twentieth century? If so, we do not know his name. Therefore we must make an effort to offer a final accounting of Ludendorff and what he wrought.

CHAPTER 11

Ludendorff and His Work

E MERGING FROM THE ashes of post–World War I Germany, the Nazis condemned the Weimar Republic for agreeing to an armistice in November 1918 that led to the signing of the Treaty of Versailles and its onerous reparations. The Nazis embraced nationalism, antiliberalism, and later anti-Semitism—all with devastating effects.

Today Nazism is associated with the most horrific events in history and has become identified with the worst parts of human nature. But why do we call Erich Ludendorff "the first Nazi"?

In *The Guns of August,* her Pulitzer Prize–winning history of the prelude to the First World War, Barbara Tuchman wrote that even though Ludendorff was given more power than any German since Frederick the Great, the descriptions of him were incomplete and the man has remained a mystery. Consequently, to understand Ludendorff, we have had to piece together threads of evidence and scattered clues he left behind.

With any historical person, we would normally look to the family for hints, but Ludendorff had no real family. He had stepsons through his marriage with his first wife, but two of them died in his offensives. He showed regret that they were dead and had their bodies moved to a stately crypt in a Berlin church, but that was all. His third stepson helped in his failed Hitler–Ludendorff coup of 1923, but that boy then faded from view and was heard no more.

Researching the rest of Ludendorff's family tells nothing. H. L. Mencken, the famed American journalist, researched each of Ludendorff's brothers. One brother, Richard, lived in the Dutch West Indies, but when contacted he had nothing to say about Ludendorff. Another brother, Eugene, was a government official who once worked in Aix-la-Chapelle, but again Mencken could get no material from him. A third brother, Hans Ludendorff, majored in the astronomy of the ancient Mayans and became a first-rate astronomer. One wonders if the obscurity of his profession were a result of his trying to distance himself from his famous sibling. He told nothing about his brother, and he buried himself in ancient texts. His best books were meticulous catalogues of various aster- oids and stars, plus digressions about the Mayans before Columbus. Only one was translated into English, and that is safely held by the great archives of Harvard and barely anyplace else.

Ludendorff had a sister, Madame Jahn, who was married to an official in the German Treasury. But Ludendorff disowned her when she ridiculed his tirades against the Masons. She told him Masons were harmless, and Ludendorff insisted that they were a bloodthirsty clan. He wrote an eighty-two-page booklet warning of their danger. In it he argued that the top Masonic lodge in New York City had persuaded Woodrow Wilson to declare war against Germany, thus causing Ludendorff to lose the war. This booklet sold almost 100,000 copies.

Ludendorff's first wife, Margarethe Pernet, was the clean-cut daughter of a factory owner. She tried to be a supportive partner to

Ludendorff, but under his influence, she became melancholic and succumbed to morphine. He divorced her and placed her in an asylum. She died when she was only sixty-one years old, locked up like a prisoner.

Ludendorff did seem fonder of his second wife, Mathilde von Kemnitz, and we know that he was grateful for how she codified his ideas. She put down on paper his tirades against Masons and Catholics and various other Christians. She became crazed with the idea that Jews were attacking Germany and that the power behind the Jews was the Dalai Lama of Tibet. Indeed, she was the one who seems to have convinced him that the Masons in New York City had gotten America to declare war on Germany in 1917. And it was she who tried to put together a synthesis of Ludendorff's religious ideas and who helped Ludendorff become anti-Christian.

Mathilde came up with the compelling slogan "Are you a Christian or are you a German?" and she went on to develop Ludendorff's love of the old Germanic gods, particularly Woden. After the Second World War she pretended that she and her husband had been secretly against the Nazis, even though Ludendorff had led the Nazis as their first (coalition) candidate for the presidency of Germany in 1925. She started a special institute to promote her religious ideas, the Foundation for God Knowledge, but the West German government shut it down on January 8, 1951, in its drive against neo-Nazis. She pretended, in vain, that she and her husband had been anti-Nazi at heart, but prosecutors insisted that she and he had been instrumental in bringing Hitler to power.

All in all we learn little from both wives. Ludendorff's first wife wrote a memoir, but it was very guarded and was clear only in its criticisms of Mathilde.

It would be wonderful if we could know information from the parents and grandparents of Ludendorff. What little is known has been summarized earlier. His father was patriotic, and the house was filled with books and prints about Germany's successes against Austria in 1866 and France in 1870. Such items could have been found in the majority of German homes of the era and would have been unsurprising in any of them.

So again we are left a man without a shadow. And making an evaluation of Ludendorff's life is further complicated because he was a sly man who spun legends about himself, myths that kept changing. Amid all this, one fact stands above the others: General Erich Ludendorff was the source of more widespread damage than practically any other man of his time. Lenin, Stalin, and Hitler were certainly of great importance. Ludendorff, however, was hardly far beneath them in impact. He increased the pain and suffering in the First World War by pushing gas warfare, by demanding something not far from genocide in conquered territory, and by insisting on total victory when compromise was an option. When he sent Lenin to Russia in a sealed train in 1917, Ludendorff set into motion events that would spread Communism to battered countries in too many corners of the world.

The stab-in-the-back legend that Ludendorff created offered the justification for overthrowing the Weimar Republic, and it was integral to Hitler's rise to power. The revered Holger Herwig has called this legend "the first step on the road to Auschwitz." We have no doubt that this is true.

One amazing example of Ludendorff's impact can be seen in the early 1940s during World War II, a few years after his death. In January 1943, at the Casablanca Conference, Roosevelt and

Churchill agreed that they should make it impossible for Germans ever to pretend that they had not been defeated. As Professor Roger Chickering put it, "Roosevelt and Churchill understood that Germany had not been resoundingly defeated at the end of World War I. They wanted every German to know at the end of World War II that they *had* been defeated, and unconditionally." Their idea made sense in 1943, but the two great men may have unintentionally prolonged the war with this effort. British military historian J. F. C. Fuller noted, "Unconditional Surrender crippled opposition to Hitler within Germany and, like a blood transfusion, gave two years further life to the war."

German Luftwaffe field marshal Albert Kesselring and Wehrmacht field marshal Erich von Manstein agreed. General Hasso von Manteuffel responded to the Casablanca Conference announcement with the summation: "We must fight to the bitter end with the courage of desperation." He added: "The demand for Unconditional Surrender welded workers and soldiers together in a way that amazed me." With this demand, the Allies became prisoners of their noble idea that to avoid another stab-in-the-back legend, they had to defeat Germany utterly.

After a German colonel tried to assassinate Hitler on July 20, 1944, with a briefcase bomb, the SS collected information on all the possible dissidents in Germany and found that more than 4,000 of them—influential men and women noted for their intelligence, power, means, or prestige—might want to reach out and make peace with the English and Americans. But the doctrine of unconditional surrender from the Casablanca Conference made it impossible for any Allied intelligence person to negotiate with such people, and the dissidents had to be silent. Many of them had to die.

A case can be made that due to Ludendorff's stab-in-the-back legend, which led to the Second World War, the Allies' doctrine of unconditional surrender extended that war by at least a year, perhaps even leading to the Pacific Theater and Hiroshima, though making this connection can incite controversy.

Let us note here that the Allies' insistence on getting the Nazis to surrender unconditionally contributed momentum to getting the Japanese to do the same. And the Japanese could not do so because such a surrender meant that they could not guarantee the existence of their beloved emperor. Therefore they had to fight on. And this in turn caused Americans to drop atomic bombs to get the proper surrender from them.

In the springtime of 1945, when the Nazis were collapsing, the Allies were looking for a bridge over the Rhine to transport their tanks and armored columns into the heart of Germany. One bridge, at a place called Remagen, was still standing and fit the bill. It seemed that here God had a sense of humor: The locals had named the overpass Ludendorff Bridge because Ludendorff had built it in World War I to channel traffic for his deadly offensives. Ludendorff had had it built in 1916 by captive Russian soldiers. Now on March 7, 1945, as the Americans approached, Hitler ordered this bridge destroyed. His soldiers put a gigantic demolition charge on the structure, but a lucky shell from an American tank of the Ninth Armored Division shredded the fuse. The charge was neutralized, and then up swarmed the brave men of that division, killing every German in sight and capturing the structure. Hitler went berserk and attempted to blow up the structure with frogmen, artillery, and rockets, all with his usual incompetence and all to no avail. Now the passage to Germany was taken, and that land was open to defeat.

German generals, learning that Americans were crossing the Rhine over Ludendorff Bridge, saw that they had lost the war. The Allies were pouring into the center of the nation. Ludendorff Bridge now symbolized the fall of the blood-soaked Third Reich. Ludendorff's name became a symbol of the end of the world war, to which he had made such terrible contributions.

Yet for all his evil, Ludendorff receives no blame today. Hitler and Stalin receive increasing credit for their crimes, but Ludendorff is forgotten in an obscure cemetery in Bavaria. That he remains nearly unknown in the United States, after murdering millions, is due to several factors. First, subsequent generations in the Untied States were not clear regarding most of the early twentieth century in Europe. Then America went into a massive isolation in the 1920s and 1930s, when Ludendorff and Hitler were doing some of their major and most damaging work. That added to the confusion. Also, values in the interwar years were askew. Here the case of Lenin and Kerensky is instructive. Kerensky gave Russia its first free government, gave women the vote before any other country in Europe, and started Russia on the path to democracy. Yet the average American sports star has greater recognition. When Kerensky died in 1970, most people did not know who he was, and the few who did despised him. He had to be buried almost anonymously in London, so unpopular was he in Russian exile circles in the United States.

Meanwhile Lenin, the tyrant who killed millions, is given the respect due a pharaoh and lies in a granite tomb in the center of Moscow. Every year, 1,000,000 respectful people visit his carefully preserved corpse, dressed in a custom-tailored suit imported from London.

Ludendorff, who probably killed nearly as many as Lenin, never got credit for extending World War I, for the military's use of

poison gas, for bankrolling Lenin's rise to power, or for helping kill
the German politicians who signed the peace he demanded in 1918.
He pushed the world toward World War II yet never got credit for
that either.

What is remarkable here is how good Ludendorff and his circle were at spreading propaganda and disinformation in his favor.
In the 1930s, Ludendorff and his aides disseminated a considerable amount of rot to make people think better of him. Even
modern historians have been fooled. In a celebrated telegram that
Ludendorff was reported to have sent in 1933 to Hindenburg, after
that man included Hitler in his government, Ludendorff is said to
have warned Hindenburg: "By appointing Hitler Chancellor of the
Reich, you have handed over our sacred German Fatherland to one
of the greatest demagogues of all time. I prophesy to you that this
evil man will plunge our Reich into the abyss and will inflict im-
measurable woe on our nation. Future generations will curse you in
your grave for this action."

The telegram makes Ludendorff into a visionary, selflessly
giving up his past ideas to honor the truth. He becomes a Don
Quixote who, after living the life of a crazy man, dies a wise one.
And that seems superlative. But the problem is that the telegram
is false—it was almost certainly concocted by him and his followers to redeem his reputation. There is no copy of the telegram in the sprawling Hindenburg archives, and no one in the
Hindenburg administration ever remembered seeing it. Nor has
any historian found confirmation of it. Yet more than a dozen
major historians have accepted the telegram as truth, including
Spencer Tucker in his 816-page tome *The European Powers in
the First World War*, which declares: "By the time of his death in

Munich on December 20, 1937, Ludendorff was warning about Hitler's tyranny.' "

Tucker, a first-rate scholar, is not alone. The famed Nazi expert Sir Ian Kershaw was taken in with the tale of Ludendorff's final position against Hitler, and he recorded it in several of his histories, until he later recognized the story as a lie and corrected the error. In subsequent publications of his fine books, the forged telegram does not appear. The false telegram, however, has whitewashed Ludendorff to others who lack Kershaw's wide expertise, and it has reduced the world's awareness of his abominations.

A final reason why so few know of Ludendorff's terrible acts is is that World War II came so soon after World War I, and this made it difficult for historians to thoroughly examine the issues at leisure. General John Eisenhower, son of General Dwight D. Eisenhower, once argued that it takes thirty years to have the dust settle and get a full assessment of how a war happened. After other wars, there was time for historians to make this kind of judgment. But because World War II began not long after the First World War ended, the historian's focus turned to Hitler and the Nazis.

It took the efforts of more than two dozen nations to destroy Hitler. And then, in 1945, when the war was over, Germany became an ally of the United States, and American historians never really examined Germany's full record in detail. They saw Germany as a new democracy and saw Hitler as an aberration, one that started in the 1930s. Both historian Rod Paschall and military historian Edward M. Coffman of the University of Wisconsin–Madison and editor at the Weider History Group agree on this. The mass of information on Hitler and World War II drowned out any quiet examination of Ludendorff and World War I.

This is a pity because Ludendorff's life is key to understanding the twentieth century. In fact, no one can understand Hitler without first understanding Ludendorff—one came ideologically from the world of the other. Ludendorff contributed many of the traditions that made Hitler possible. How many people understand that Ludendorff created a rationale that justified the Holocaust?

As British historian Hugh Trevor Roper once noted, "History is not merely what happened. It is what happened in the context of what might have been." So to fully understand Ludendorff and his legacy, let us imagine what kind of world we might have had if this man had never existed. Let us imagine that he had been shot in 1914 during the first days of World War I, when he was in Belgium. The changes in the last century would have been major.

Without Ludendorff, Lenin could have stayed in Zurich, and Communism could have withered on the vine, without reaching Russia. The Russians would have had Kerensky and a flourishing Russian democracy. In a letter to a Communist economist named Yevgeni Preobrazhensky, Trotsky wrote: "You know better than I do that had Lenin not managed to come to Saint Petersburg, the October Revolution would not have taken place."

Possibly no one would have held out for a total victory as Ludendorff did, and there might have been a gentler peace for all, achieved sooner. If so, the fall of so many dynasties of Europe might not have taken place and the war could have ended sooner, without such devastation in Europe.

And without Ludendorff, there might have been no Hitler, because Ludendorff's stab-in-the-back legend helped make Hitler's program conceivable. Additionally, Ludendorff's running for the presidency of Germany under a coalition arrangement with Hitler gave Hitler a legitimacy that otherwise he would have lacked. Very possibly, without it, Hitler would not have come to power.

So we must make the case that this man is almost equal in importance to Hitler and Stalin. Indeed, one wonders whether without him there would have been a Second World War. World War II was "the unnecessary war," as Churchill called it, a war that did not need to happen. Without Ludendorff's myths, which made Hitler's beliefs plausible, the Nazis might never have been able to come to power.

Most analyses of World War II tend to begin with Hitler. And most people assume that Nazism began with that man. But it was Ludendorff who unleashed the social, military, and political forces that were key to Hitler's success. And it is due to Ludendorff's fundamental influence on men like Hitler, plus the devastating consequences of his convictions and actions, that we can argue that in an abstract sense, the first Nazi was Ludendorff.

Historians have not really seen Ludendorff for all he was, and this is hardly their fault. There was not sufficient access to many historical records until the explosion of the Internet. Only recently has it been possible to place Erich Ludendorff squarely in the pantheon of historical figures who not only influenced the events of World War I for Germany, but also had massive influence beyond, into the dynamics of World War II and the overall evolution of Western civilization.

—*The End*—

Timeline of the Great War

1914

JUNE 28: An Austrian archduke is shot in Serbia.

JULY 5: Germany supports Austria in its ultimatum against Serbia.

JULY 23: Austria and Serbia confer, and Austria is not satisfied.

JULY 31: Germany sees Russia backing Serbia.

AUGUST 1: Germany declares war on Russia.

AUGUST 3–4: Germany is at war with France, Belgium, and the United Kingdom.

AUGUST 4: Germany invades Belgium on an impossibly strict timetable.

AUGUST 4–16: Germany gets bogged down in Belgium, and the timetable is broken.

AUGUST 17: Russia invades Germany ahead of schedule.

AUGUST 23–30: The Battle of Tannenberg. Germany sees this as a great victory. But Germany is bogging down everywhere, and the conflict is now a war of attrition, the one kind Germany cannot win.

1915

APRIL 22: Germans use poison gas, which effects gigantic slaughters.

MAY 7: Germans start unrestricted submarine warfare, which enrages Americans.

SEPTEMBER 11: The British start developing tank warfare. The war is gratuitous murder everywhere, with few results.

1916

FEBRUARY 21: The Battle of Verdun begins. One million will die.

JUNE 4: The Russians launch the Brusilov Offensive in a desperate effort to find a way out of the war. Each side suffers almost 1,000,000 casualties.

AUGUST 29: Hindenburg is made chief of staff, and Ludendorff is made first quartermaster general. The Duo is now firmly in power, and they eclipse the Kaiser.

1917

JANUARY 19: The United States, exasperated by the Zimmermann Telegram and unrestricted submarine warfare, declares war on Germany. This is Ludendorff's greatest fiasco to date. Soon, "The Yanks are coming."

MARCH 15: The Russian government falls, ending a dynasty some 300 years old.

APRIL 16: Ludendorff gets Lenin to Russia.

JUNE 25: Far ahead of schedule, American soldiers begin to arrive in Europe. Soon they arrive at a rate above 100,000 per month. Ludendorff refuses to understand this is a pure disaster; he orders a blackout of any news about the Yanks being in Europe.

JULY 1: Kerensky tries to maintain Russian obligations and launches the Kerensky Offensive.

JULY 19: The Kerensky Offensive collapses and the Russian army dies.

NOVEMBER 1: The Russian October Revolution explodes.

NOVEMBER 20: The British use tanks in force for the first time. Germans scatter.

DECEMBER – MARCH: Ludendorff tries to force Russians to sign a humiliating peace at Brest-Litovsk.

1918

MARCH 2: The Germans advance in the East and threaten Kiev.

MARCH 3: Trotsky signs the peace treaty, in tears.

MARCH 21–AUGUST 6: Ludendorff conducts the Ludendorff Offensives.

MARCH 26: General Foch of France is made supreme commander and lets the Germans advance while hitting them on all sides.

JULY 17: Americans attack at Château-Thierry.

AUGUST 6: Ludendorff makes one last offensive and fails.

AUGUST 8: "The Black Day of the German Army." German soldiers are drunk, insubordinate, and cynical, and they shout all manner of discouraging words to any advancing German troops. They only want to go home.

AUGUST 21: The Allies break the German line at multiple points, and Ludendorff can only do stopgap measures.

SEPTEMBER 30: Bulgaria, one of Germany's allies, surrenders.

OCTOBER: Ludendorff is mercurial, waxing optimistic and then fatalistic. Finally he makes a histrionic resignation, and on October 29, the Kaiser is glad to accept it. Interestingly, Hindenburg makes no objection.

OCTOBER 17: The Allies break through the Hindenburg Line.

OCTOBER 29: The German Navy mutinies.

OCTOBER 30: The Ottoman Empire, allied to Germany, surrenders.

NOVEMBER 4: The Austrians, allied to Germany, make peace with Italy.

NOVEMBER 9: The Kaiser abdicates.

NOVEMBER 10: Charles I of Austria abdicates.

NOVEMBER 11: At the eleventh hour on the eleventh day of the eleventh month, the war is over. It had been called "the war to end all wars," but soldiers now call it "the war to end all men."

NOVEMBER–JANUARY: Ludendorff puts on a disguise, flees the country, writes his memoirs, spreads the stab-in-the-back legend, and blames the Jews for everything.

1919

JANUARY 18–JUNE 28: The Allies negotiate a severe peace with Germany, but it is no worse than what Germany had inflicted on Russia at Brest. Peace is signed on June 28, the fifth anniversary of the assassination of Archduke Ferdinand in Sarajevo.

JANUARY ONWARD: Ludendorff plots revenge, sponsors Hitler, and rants like a madman. Overall he justifies the Nazis, gives them respectability, and makes them credible with the stab-in-the-back legend, thus paving the way to a new war.

The Cast of Characters

ARCHDUKE FERDINAND

The visit of Archduke Franz Ferdinand to the town of Sarajevo started the war. This is what happened:

(1) Ferdinand was important. He was heir to the throne of Austria-Hungary.

(2) But he married a commoner.

(3) The court did not approve and gave his wife no respect.

(4) Indeed, at important functions she was not even permitted to sit with him.

(5) The only way he could show her a good time was to travel around as the inspector general of the armies of Austria. On those trips, she was treated like a grand lady.

(6) On June 28, 1914, they went to Sarajevo, to inspect the army there.

(7) Ferdinand looked grand, for he was sewn into his uniform.

(8) He took two bullets, shot by a student named Princip. Ferdinand died because the doctors took too much time figuring out that his tunic had to be cut off.

(9) With his death, the Austrians declared war on Serbia, a nation backed by Russia. Russia declared war on Austria, a nation backed by Germany . . . and then the dominos began to fall. One point here should be noted: Germany wanted war with Russia. The German military gurus told the Kaiser that Russia was getting strong—so strong that if war were not declared by 1923, Russia would become invincible and would be able to destroy Germany.

BERNSTORFF

Count Heinrich von Bernstorff was the able German ambassador to the United States who knew America's resources. He kept telling the Germans to keep out of war with the United States, to no avail. Most Germans believed that the US Army was minute and therefore unimportant, but this mind-set was fatal to Germans like the Kaiser and later Hitler. Bernstorff tried and failed to convince anyone of importance. Eventually he gave up and moved to Switzerland. It would take two world wars for Germany to learn to respect the United States.

Bernstorff was married to a German-American woman who taught him about the United States. He wrote two memoirs. He was a progressive Anglophile, and he scorned the Machiavellian style of Bismarck. Hitler despised him and when he came to power, the diplomat was lucky to be living in exile.

BLOCH

Jean de Bloch was the one visionary who realized that there was no way for war to be won by anyone in 1914. There was a guaranteed stalemate. The power of defense was so great that no one side could win. How could men be brave against 1,000 miles of barbed wire and machine gun fire? Note that only Churchill deeply understood this, and he therefore pushed the development of the tank, an invention that lifted the siege.

BRUSILOV

Aleksei Brusilov was the forgotten hero of the Allies, the Russian general whom Churchill praised to the skies. He conducted a brilliant offensive against the Austrians; it hurt them so badly that they were never an offensive force thereafter. Had he been supported, and not sabotaged, he could have saved Russia from revolution. When the revolution did break out, he worked for the revolutionaries and ably so.

See Churchill's book about the Russian front, *The Forgotten War*, for more about him. Strangely, he dedicated his memoir, *A Soldier's Notebook*, to the Kaiser, who then returned the favor and dedicated his to Brusilov.

CASEMENT

Sir Roger Casement was a prestigious Irish crusader who did more to protect South American Indians than nearly anyone in his time. Indeed, he saved thousands of battered Peruvian Indians from destruction. Later he tried to raise a Rebel Brigade of Irish prisoners of war in Germany to fight for Irish independence. He was captured and executed by the British. The British neutralized his positive work for Germany and Ireland by proving, to the world's satisfaction, that he was a pervert who wanted to bed young boys in South America and South Africa.

CHURCHILL

Winston Churchill's work in World War I is underemphasized and misunderstood. He put together a plan to destroy the German allies, sending an expedition to Gallipoli to destroy Turkey. It was a sublime plan, but it failed because it was misapplied and because it was resisted by the greatest Turk of modern times, Mustafa Kemal Atatürk, who said to his men, "I do not order you to fight. I order you to die." Churchill then put together a strategy using tanks, which did win the war. He constantly said that Communism was a plague to be extirpated, and he wanted an Allied invasion of Russia at war's end, but people thought him a fanatic and did not respect him sufficiently until later.

For a better understanding of Churchill, read the one novel he wrote, *Savrola*, which tells about his inner mind and personality. Churchill was, all in all, the most impressive and successful man of the century. The awesome mystery is that he often saw himself as a failure, perhaps because he had to preside over the liquidation of the British Empire.

CLEMENCEAU

Georges Clemenceau was the greatest Frenchman of the age. He was a rarity, a Frenchman who understood America. He had lived in America and had even married one of his students when he taught there. He had also worked in America as a journalist. He played his American card perfectly, holding France together till the Yanks arrived. He overcame the partial mutinies of the French Army, difficulties with the British, and the collapse of the Russians. He would have continued the struggle even if Paris had fallen. Somehow Ludendorff never understood this.

CONRAD VON HÖTZENDORF

General Franz Conrad von Hötzendorf was the top Austrian general and was perhaps the most overestimated officer of the Central Powers. He never realized that his nation was a decomposing corpse and never stood up to the bloody demands of his German ally. Unfathomably, he continues to enjoy a positive reputation.

DULLES

Allen Dulles was an experienced diplomat. As an observer, he was often excellent. His early years in Switzerland, during and after World War I, gave him extraordinary vantage points. He was the individual who took Lenin's call at the US Embassy, just before Ludendorff sent Lenin to Russia. Later he was the CIA spy who grew that agency from its infancy. Because his brother became secretary of state, there was never sufficient oversight of that agency in its early years, and this tragic confluence meant that the agency grew without disciplined supervision. He succeeded in much of his work. As for the Korean War, he never sensed its approach, even with the warnings from the Korean chief of state, Syngman Rhee, who swore it was coming. At the Bay of Pigs in Cuba, he presided over the worst US military fiasco in the Americas.

FALKENHAYN

Erich von Falkenhayn was the one general in Germany at the top who did not want it all. He realized that to be strong everywhere is to be strong nowhere. He wanted to win on one front, make peace, and go home. He was the best top general in Germany, and he erred just once: He decided that the ideal approach would be to beat France at Verdun. This effort failed badly, killed 1,000,000, and discredited him utterly.

Had he sent German forces east with the same effort, they could have taken Saint Petersburg, and history could have been different. He was sacked after Verdun and was sent to command troops in Transylvania, then Palestine. In Palestine he saved countless Jews from Arabs but then faded from view.

For more, see his book *Critical Decisions at General Headquarters*, published in 1919.

FRANÇOIS

General Hermann von François was a brilliant German general who, behind the scenes, did the real planning and work that won at Tannenberg. On three separate occasions he disobeyed orders— orders that would have led to disaster—and he was responsible for the decisive victory. Later he said as much. After the war, he took friends on a tour of the battlefield and said three things: "Here is where General Hindenburg slept before the battle . . . here is where Hindenburg slept after the battle . . . and here, God damn it, is where Hindenburg slept *during* the battle!"

GÖRING

Hermann Göring was the most incompetent German general of World War II. A drug addict, sexual deviant, and amazingly eccentric person, he was capable of showing up for a funeral wearing a mink coat, a white-and-black military uniform, and makeup. US ambassador William Christian Bullitt, the American representative in France, said in the 1930s that he looked like a pimp in a bordello.

Somehow this man became head of the German Air Force at the end of World War I and then became Hitler's best friend. He was the only man allowed to call Hitler by the familiar *Du,* and even asked Hitler to be the best man at his wedding.

Many Allied officers give him credit for losing World War II. It was he who made the mistakes that allowed the British to escape at Dunkirk. It was he who made the errors that lost Stalingrad. And finally he lost Normandy.

His one strength was understanding how to ride the waves of power. When he was at Nuremberg, he lost his case and was condemned to die, but he managed to die easily, in silk pajamas, taking a poison that a doctor had hidden under a layer of skin.

He kept Hitler ignorant about the growing weaknesses of the German Air Force and in this way served the Allies enormously, without knowing it. Some visionaries in England have said that the British owed him a medal for having contributed so wonderfully to Allied victory.

HANNIBAL

Hannibal, the general of antiquity, was ever an inspiration to the German military. All German military plans, from the middle 1800s to the 1940s, were predicated in some form on the idea of encircling the enemy and then using all available troops to fight and destroy him. The hope was that if they had 100 percent of their troops fanned out around the enemy, and if the enemy did not have all his troops in contact with these troops, then one could destroy even a superior enemy.

Hitler tried to use this maneuver in his invasion of Russia, and at first it was successful. But ultimately it failed at Stalingrad.

Had Germans not been so fixated on Hannibal's maneuvers, they would not have believed in their ability to win speedy victories and a two-front war. It was Hannibal's ideas that gave German officers the conviction that victory was in their grasp. They believed this even though most Hannibal-type maneuvers of encirclement have failed, throughout history.

Intriguingly, Hannibal was defeated by a Roman emperor named Fabian, and George Washington was called an American Fabian. Fabian delayed and let Hannibal overextend himself, and then he destroyed him bit by bit.

The Allies under the French general Foch did exactly that to Ludendorff during the ill-fated Ludendorff Offensives, and it cost Ludendorff the war.

HINDENBURG

Hindenburg was an old retired general in his seventies who came back to life in 1914 and got credit for the German victory at Tannenberg. During the war he became senile, and Ludendorff took over command. He never disagreed with Ludendorff except during the last month of the war.

What is remarkable is the way he came under Ludendorff's influence. At the beginning of the war, Hindenburg had no territorial ambitions for Germany and did not talk of indemnities. But by the end, he was as greedy as Ludendorff. Ultimately he fell entirely under the influence of Ludendorff.

HITLER

Adolf Hitler is a rich source of controversy among biographers. The Israeli Mossad got its hands on the Russian autopsy of his body and discovered that the man had only one testicle. The photos of him as a child show deranged-looking eyes, perhaps revealing what was in his mind. Canaris, the German admiral, felt that Hitler was made mad by World War I and the poison gases, which Ludendorff introduced onto the battlefield. But this cannot be confirmed.

When Ludendorff began to blame the Jews for Germany's defeat in World War I, Hitler said he wanted the Jews to be gassed the same way that German soldiers had been gassed in that war. One wonders what life he would have led if Ludendorff had not given him the idea of blaming the Jews. Hitler was talented with watercolors; perhaps he could have been a high school art teacher.

All the Nazi elites who were veterans of World War I have one thing in common: they all, without exception, became nostalgic over that war, and they wanted to reenact it because it was their shining hour. This was nostalgia with a vengeance.

Of course additional factors made Hitler the man he became. Some first-rate theologians are convinced that Hitler was possessed by the devil. Note that their evidence suggests that this might also be the case for just two other men in recent centuries: Marx and Napoleon. Of these three, the case for Marx is the strongest.

KAISER WILHELM II

Kaiser Wilhelm II was a damaged man from the day he was born—
it took his mother more than twelve hours to deliver him, and the
delivery damaged him badly. One of his hands was mangled and
never grew long enough. His knowledge of world affairs was thin—
it seems he followed only two experts: He went along with Darwin
and thought Germany would have to achieve the "survival of the
fittest." And he went along with US admiral Alfred Thayer Mahan
and thought Germany would have to develop a gigantic surface
fleet to menace England. His limited knowledge did him harm.
From Mahan he learned to love only surface ships and thus took
no great interest in submarines. When war came, he never could use
his ships, and the submarines were in perilously short supply. From
Darwin he learned a dangerous bluster—that is, a survival-of-the-
fittest philosophy, which alienated Russia and England.

With stronger allies and with more submarines and more diplomacy, he might have avoided, or even won, a war.

KERENSKY

Fyodor Kerensky was a fine professor who had no training in deal-
ing with a ghoul like Lenin. He is often remembered harshly, but in
truth, he was the most democratic leader of Russia in his century.
He is scorned for continuing the war, but he knew that if he made
peace with Ludendorff, the Allies might be finished. He is despised
by many for making his army too democratic, whereby men could
vote on the orders they would accept. But he knew that the army
was so close to mutiny that he had few options.

History despises losers. There will never be a good word for
Louis XVI even though he was a better man than Napoleon. There

will never be a good word for Nicholas II even though he was better than Stalin. And there will never be a good word for Kerensky even though he was superior to Lenin.

Students of power, like Dr. Henry Kissinger, despise Kerensky. Once, in a dispute with an ineffective Portuguese premier, Kissinger hissed, "You are going to be a Kerensky."

"I do not want to be a Kerensky," the man responded.

"Neither did Kerensky," Kissinger answered.

LEMKIN

Raphael Lemkin was the battered Polish lawyer who came to America, talked about the slaughter of the Jews, and invented the word *genocide*. A tragic figure, he lost all capacity for anything except warning people about genocide, and he lived in poverty, spoke just a tad too severely, and became consumed with his crusade. No one paid attention to him, and he was unknown. Yet he was a man of greatness.

He lectured occasionally at Yale, Rutgers, and the University of Virginia. He explained that genocide was not just the act of killing a people. It was, rather, an effort to destroy a people "in whole or in part."

Lemkin came to America when he learned that the Polish government of the 1920s and '30s did not approve of him and, finally, was resisting him. He was a prophet without honor in his own country.

When he died, only seven people came to the funeral. Yet he achieved much: He called attention to the genocidal attempts against Armenians, Jews, and Ukrainians. Samantha Power, Harvard's expert on genocide, endorses this man without reservations.

LENIN

Lenin is perhaps the most overrated man of his century. His discipline was strong. His ability to instill terror was decided. His ability to give glib phrases to gloss over his crimes was still greater. For example, take the slogan "Freedom is so precious it must be rationed."

Still, there is not much of a difference between Lenin and Stalin, except that Lenin was more efficient. For more on this, see Aleksandr Solzhenitsyn's *The Gulag Archipelago* and Roy Medvedev's *Let History Judge* and evaluate Lenin's taking of hostages, his punishment of adversaries merely because they might go against him, and his terrorizing of minorities merely because they might disagree with him, and then compare this behavior to the behavior of Stalin. The two are then alike. The difference is but one of scale.

Lenin had syphilis, and his body was burdened by medicines he took to cope with it. Further, he had been shot by two bullets that were tipped with arsenic, and this also poisoned his system. His biggest achievements were that he was a man of staggering concentration and that he was the most effective terrorist of the century.

LLOYD GEORGE

Prime Minister David Lloyd George was the ace politician of the United Kingdom who, in Hitler's view, caused the Allies to win World War I. He seems to have made only one major error: In 1918 he was so exasperated with the way the British generals were spending the lives of their soldiers that he began to keep the British army in France undersupplied with men, so that they would lose fewer of them. So when Ludendorff attacked, the British army was in worse straits than it would have been otherwise. But somehow the understrength British divisions snatched victory out of the jaws of defeat.

Lloyd George was a brilliant Welshman. His hero was Abraham Lincoln, after whom he patterned his life.

LUDENDORFF

Erich Ludendorff was, ultimately, a disciplined but mediocre entity. He spent his years studying one thing, tactics, and he never gave himself time for friends, love, or children. He also never learned how to seek out unpleasant truths and was always surrounded by sycophants who told him what he wanted to hear. He was much like the world-famous chess player Bobby Fischer, who spent so many years studying chess that he became destabilized and insane. Fisher became so demented that he, a Jew, decided that the Holocaust did not take place. Ludendorff became so demented that he felt that he had won World War I but had been sabotaged by Jews.

For more on Ludendorff, see Karl Tschuppik's *Ludendorff, the Tragedy of a Military Mind*. Unfortunately, this book closes Ludendorff's story around 1932 and does not go into his full contributions to the Nazis. But it does go into his persona very well.

NICHOLAS II

Nicholas II of Russia made errors that lost both his war and his nation. First, he appointed himself chief of the army, thus bringing upon himself the penalties for any lost battle. Second, he abolished his major source of income by eliminating his alcohol monopoly in the middle of the war. Third, he never sufficiently supported his one great general, Aleksei Brusilov. Fourth, he embraced the madness of Grigori Rasputin. Fifth, he allowed Communist literature into

Russia because he believed that it was so crazy that no one would take it seriously. Sixth, he never delved deeply enough into who was murdering whom in his state. He should have discovered who murdered his ablest minister, Pyotr Stolypin. This morass of errors doomed Russia.

Nicholas's famous last words, when told he was about to be shot, were pathetic: "What? What?"

PERSHING

General Pershing was a brilliant man, first in his class at West Point, like his friend Douglas MacArthur. He, like Teddy Roosevelt and French general Mangin, wanted the Allied armies to advance to Berlin and prove to the Germans that they had been beaten. But this conflicted with the mind-set of President Wilson, a southerner whose father had been a Confederate officer and who believed that the gentler the peace, the better the chance that it would endure. This can work with men like Robert E. Lee, but not with the likes of Ludendorff or Hitler.

PRINCIP

Few blame Gavrilo Princip for the outbreak of the world war—it is often suggested that the war was an accident looking for a place to happen. But if Princip had not fired that shot in 1914, the war would have happened later. And if the war had happened later, there is every chance that the Russians would have been able to make a better showing of themselves. The famed English historian Alistair Horne states unequivocally in *Verdun: The Price of Valor* that had the war happened later, the Russians could have won. By 1914 Russia was improving by leaps and bounds. The planned rail links to Archangel and Murmansk would have made it far easier to receive supplies from England and the United States. The improvements being made in the Russian Army would have had time to develop.

From this angle, Princip is the most effective assassin in modern times. Only the Arab who shot Bob Kennedy and changed history by putting Nixon in the White House is as important.

RADEK

Karl Radek has been remembered as the last Communist internationalist. When the Communist elites were scrambling for privilege and luxuries, Radek was the only one idealistic enough to ask for no favors. Indeed, the ugly beard he wore was a necessity because he never asked for extra firewood or coal to heat his chilly apartment.

Radek should be remembered for his flashes of genius. It was he who dominated the writing of the journal *The Torch*, which was distributed in multiple languages to the German troops occupying Russia—and this work neutralized them as no military power could have done. And it was Radek who called for a real, international Communism, while his peers took refuge in a chauvinist Russian creed that was to dominate the movement for decades.

Radek was so brilliant that he seems to have dominated the ghouls who got him ready for the show trials of Stalin. He snapped to them that he was big enough to take them down too. He threatened to confess to being part of a great international plot and to say that his captors were part of his treason. Suddenly the ghouls realized Radek could get them killed, and they began to sweat. Radek then insisted that they figure out some way to have him merely sentenced to years in the camps in Siberia.

This succeeded brilliantly. When he heard the sentence read out, the international journalists saw him smile with relief. It was, absolutely, one of the few triumphs for those being butchered by Stalin.

Stalin of course did catch up to Radek. Evidence indicates that he was killed in the camps in 1939 at Stalin's orders.

REED

Jack Reed was a true believer, an absolutely devoted Communist. But hard-core zealots like Grigory Zinoviev distrusted him and sent him off to the town of Baku in the Crimea, to represent the party at a pan-Islam conference there.

On the way to the conference, by train, Reed was amazed to see the delegates receiving a pack of beautiful teenage whores, delivered by a cluster of aged female panders. The whores came aboard the train in fur coats and were naked underneath.

Reed had no problem with free love. But to whore these innocent girls was unthinkable. Yet the delegates were doing just that. It was arrogant, vicious, indeed Stalinist. This, and the vain luxuries of the delegates, broke Reed's heart, and he returned to Moscow in pure agony of soul. He told Louise Bryant, the woman he loved, that he felt miserable that he had misunderstood and misrepresented this Communist movement.

When he got sick and died unattended in the hospital, he was very much alone. Lenin did not detach any doctors to help him. He died muttering, "Caught in a trap, caught in a trap." It was not for nothing that he was eventually called "the Lost Revolutionary."

Supposedly, his book *Ten Days That Shook the World* was appreciated in the USSR, but it was censored soon after it was published. Stalin hated the book because he was not a primary character in it, and he soon withdrew it from circulation.

In the West, the book was devoured eagerly. Interestingly, only two journals, the *New York Times* and the *London Times*, saw the weaknesses of it. Most readers were carried away by the book's spirit—one of exuberance and adventure.

ROOSEVELT

Theodore Roosevelt was old and weak in 1917. But he was the greatest living hero in America and the most popular. His only wish before he died was to lead a division in Europe. He went to his arch adversary, President Wilson, and asked for this. In return he pledged to cease all future disagreement with the president. His plan was to go to Europe at the head of some Rough Riders, fight in the trenches, and push the Allies to go to Berlin, to prove to the Germans that they were beaten.

Had his plan played out, World War II might have been avoided. The idea is one of the most fascinating might-have-beens of the twentieth century. No one, including Ludendorff and Hitler, could have pretended that Germany was never defeated.

WILSON

President Woodrow Wilson was like President Franklin D. Roosevelt in that he knew how to win a war but not how to win a peace. His failure to make a lasting and just peace after World War I is a major disaster of modern diplomacy. At the height of US power in 1918, Wilson failed to carry the day and make a peace that was effective.

But the world was asking more than one man could deliver. Wilson was seen as a messiah who could solve all and do all. No American president had the power he had at the height of his career.

His intentions were superlative. He wanted a gentle peace like what the North tried to give the South in the United States in 1865. There would be no war criminals, no vindictiveness, no trials. He wished simply to get the other side to surrender and then go home.

Books and Notes

CHAPTER 1

On Princip

Brescia, Anthony. "The Role of Gavrilo Princip." Master's thesis, St. John's University, Queens, New York, 1965.

Butcher, Tim. *The Trigger: Hunting the Assassin Who Brought the World to War*. Grove Press, New York, 2014.

Cassels, Lavender. *The Archduke and the Assassin: Sarajevo, June 28, 1914*. Stein and Day, New York, 1984.

Clark, Christopher. *Sleepwalkers: How Europe Went to War in 1914*. Harper, New York, 2013.

Dedijer, Vladimir. *Road to Sarajevo*. Simon and Schuster, New York, 1966.

Fabijancic, Tony. *Bosnia: In the Footsteps of Gavrilo Princip*. University of Alberta Press, Edmonton, 2010.

Feuerlicht, Robert Strauss. *Desperate Act*. McGraw-Hill, New York, 1968.

King, Greg. *The Assassination of the Archduke*. McGraw-Hill, New York, 1968.

Koning, Hans. *Death of a Schoolboy*. Harcourt, New York, 1974.

Lyon, James. *Serbia and the Balkan Front, 1914: The Outbreak of the Great War*. Bloomsbury, London, 2015.

McMeekin, Sean. *July 1914: Countdown to War*. Basic Books, New York, 2013.

Quarmby, Katharine. *The Priest, the Assassin and Archduke Franz Ferdinand*. Thistle, London, 2014.

Rehr, Henrik. *Terrorist: Gavrilo Princip, the Assassin Who Ignited World War I*. Graphic Universe, Minneapolis, 2015.

Smith, David James. *One Morning in Sarajevo*. Weidenfeld & Nicolson, New York, 2009.

Villiers, Peter John. *Gavrilo Princip*. Fawler Press, Oxford, 2010.

CHAPTER 2

On Kaiser Wilhelm II

Balfour, Michael. *The Kaiser and His Times*. Houghton Mifflin, Boston, 1964.

Clark, Christopher M. *Kaiser William II*. Harlow, Longman, New York, 2000.

Clay, Catrine. *King, Kaiser, Tsar: Three Royal Cousins Who Led the World to War*. Walker, New York, 2007.

Hull, Isabel Virginia. "The Entourage of Kaiser Wilhelm II." Doctoral dissertation, Yale University, New Haven, CT, 1978.

MacDonogh, Giles. *The Last Kaiser: William the Impetuous*. Weidenfeld & Nicolson, London, 2000.

Mombauer, Annika. *The Kaiser: New Research on Wilhelm II's Role in Imperial Germany*. Cambridge University Press, New York, 2003.

Retallack, James M. *Germany in the Age of Kaiser Wilhelm II*. Macmillan, New York, 1996.

Rohl, John C. G. *The Kaiser and His Court*. Cambridge University Press, New York, 1994.

Rohl, John C. G., and Nicolaus Sombart, eds. *Kaiser Wilhelm II: New Interpretations*. Cambridge University Press, New York, 1982.

Sarkin-Hughes, Jeremy. *Germany's Genocide of the Herero*. James Currey, Woodbridge, UK, 2011.

Van der Kiste, John. *Kaiser William II: Germany's Last Emperor*. Sutton, Stroud, UK, 1999.

Viereck, George Sylvester. *The Kaiser on Trial*. Greystone Press, New York, 1937.

Whittle, Tyler. *The Last Kaiser: A Biography of William II, German Emperor and King of Prussia*. Heinemann, London, 1977.

On Schlieffen and the Plan

Bucholz, Arden. *Moltke, Schlieffen, and Prussian War Planning*. St. Martin's, New York, 1991.

Cimbala, Stephen J. *Deterrence and Provocation in Crisis and War*. Pennsylvania State University Press, University Park, 1994.

Henin, Pierre Yves. *Le Plan Schlieffen: un mois de guerre, deux siecles de controverse*. Economica Press, Paris, 2012.

Herwig, Holgar H. *The Marne, 1914*. Random House, New York, 2009.

Jannen, William. *The Lions of July*. Presidio Press, Novato, CA, 1996.

Jones, Andrew L. "Debating Cannae: Delbruck, Schlieffen, and the Great War." Master's essay, East Tennessee State University, Johnson City, 2015.

Ritter, Gerhard. *The Schlieffen Plan: Critique of a Myth*. O. Wolff, London, 1958.

Schlieffen, Alfred von. *Alfred von Schlieffen's Military Writings*. Frank Cass, Portland, OR, 2003.

———. *Cannae*. Mittler, Berlin, 1936.

Stoneman, Mark R. "William Groener, Officering, and the Schlieffen Plan." Doctoral dissertation, Georgetown University, Washington, DC, 2006.

Tunstall, Graydon A. "The Schlieffen Plan." Doctoral dissertation, Rutgers University, New Brunswick, NJ, 1974.

Wallach, J. L. "Clausewitz and Schlieffen: A Study of the Impact of Their Theories on the German Conduct of the 1914–1918 and 1939–1945 Wars." Doctoral dissertation, Oxford University, 1968.

Werstler, Glenn. "Erich von Falkenhayn and the German Response to the Problem of War on Two Fronts." Master's essay, Kutztown State College, Kutztown, PA, 1980.

CHAPTER 3

On Verdun

Brown, Malcolm. *Verdun, 1916*. Temple Publishing, Charleston, SC, 1999.

Clayton, Anthony. *Paths of Glory*. Cassell, New York, 2003.

Denizot, Alain. *Verdun, 1914–1918*. Nouveaux Editions Latines, Paris, 1996.

Horne, Alistair. *The Price of Glory*. Penguin Publishers, New York, 1994.

Keegan, John. *The First World War*. Vintage, New York, 2000.

Ousby, Ian. *The Road to Verdun*. Anchor Press, New York, 2002.

Petain, Henri Philippe. *La Bataille de Verdun*. Payot Publishers, Paris, 1929.

CHAPTER 4

On Tannenberg

Gannon, James. *Stealing Secrets, Telling Lies*. Brassey's, Washington, DC, 2001.

Golovin, Nicolai N. *The Russian Campaign of 1914*. Command and General Staff School Press, Fort Leavenworth, KS, 1933.

Griffin, Oliver L. "The German Army Looks East." Doctoral dissertation, Harvard University, Cambridge, MA, 1998.

Herwig, Holger H. *The First World War*. St. Martin's Press, London, 1996.

Ironside, Edmund. *Tannenberg: The First 30 Days in East Prussia*. Blackwood, Edinburgh, 1925.

Kagan, Frederick W., and Robin Higham, eds. *The Military History of Russia*. Macmillan, Boston, 2001.

Pawly, Ronald. *The Belgian Army in World War I.* Osprey, New York, 2009.

Rigoux, Pierre. *Tannenberg 1914: Sacrifice pour la France?* Economica Press, Paris, 2010.

Roy, James Charles. *The Vanished Kingdom: Travels through the Kingdom of Prussia.* Westview Press, Boulder, CO, 1999.

Showalter, Dennis. *Tannenberg: Clash of Empires 1914.* Brassey's, Washington, DC, 2004.

Stone, Norman. *The Eastern Front, 1914–1917.* Scribner's, New York, 1975.

Sweetman, John. *Tannenberg, 1914.* Cassell, New York, 2002.

Talbot, Randy Raymond. "General Hermann von Francois and Corps-Level Operations during the Tannenberg Campaign, August, 1914." Master's thesis, Eastern Michigan University, Ypsilanti, 1999.

CHAPTER 5

On The Duo's Coming to Power

Bridgman, Jon Marshall. "The Origins of the Military Dictatorship of Hindenburg and Ludendorff." Doctoral dissertation, Stanford University, 1960.

On General Falkenhayn

Falkenhayn, Erich von. *The German General Staff and Its Decisions.* Mead, New York, 1920.

Foley, Robert. *German Strategy and the Path to Verdun: Erich von Falkenhayn and the Development of Attrition, 1870–1916.* Cambridge University Press, Cambridge, 2005.

Hilbert, Lothar. *Falkenhayn, l'homme et sa conception de l'offensive de Verdun.* Published by author, 1976.

Werstler, Glenn. "Erich von Falkenhayn and the German Response to the Problem of War on Two Fronts, 1914–1916." Master's thesis, Kutztown University of Pennsylvania, Kutztown, 1980.

CHAPTER 6

On Fritz Haber

Charles, Daniel. *Master Mind: The Rise and Fall of Fritz Haber*. Echo Press, New York, 2005.

Hager, Thomas. *The Alchemy of Air: A Jewish Genius, a Doomed Tycoon, and the Scientific Discovery That Fed the World but Fueled the Rise of Hitler*. Harmony Books, New York, 2008.

Smil, Vaclav. *Enriching the Earth*. MIT Press, Cambridge, MA, 2001.

On Jean de Bloch

Bloch, Jean de. *La Guerre*. Garland Press, New York, 1973.

Ferguson, Niall. *The Pity of War*. Basic Books, New York, 1999.

On the Brusilov Offensive

Dowling, Timothy C. *The Brusilov Offensive*. Indiana University Press, Bloomington, 2008.

Liddell Hart, B. H. *The Real War, 1914–1918*. Little Brown and Company, New York, 1930.

Sergeyev-Tsensky, Sergei. *Brusilov's Breakthrough*. Hutchinson & Company, London, 1945.

On the Campaigns of Ludendorff with Zimmermann

Boghardt, Thomas. *The Zimmermann Telegram: Intelligence, Diplomacy, and America's Entry into World War I*. Naval Institute Press, Annapolis, MD, 2012.

Protasio, John. *The Day the World Was Shocked: The Lusitania Disaster and Its Influence on the Course of World War I*. Newbury Publishers, Haverton, PA, 2011.

Reid, B. L. *The Lives of Roger Casement*. Yale University Press, New Haven, CT, 1976.

Strother, French. *Fighting Germany's Spies*. Doubleday, Garden City, NY, 1918. (This is about the Annie Larsen conspiracy.)

Tuchman, Barbara. *The Zimmermann Telegram*. Macmillan, New York, 1966.

CHAPTER 7

On Lenin, Parvus, and the Train Voyage to Petrograd

Leggett, George. *The Cheka: Lenin's Political Police*. Clarendon Press, Oxford, 1981.

Pearson, Michael. *The Sealed Train*. Putnam's, New York, 1974.

Pipes, Richard. *The Unknown Lenin*. Yale University Press, New Haven, CT, 1999.

On Alexander Kerensky

Abraham, Richard. *Alexander Kerensky: First Love of the Revolution*. Columbia University Press, New York, 1987.

Fontenot, Michael F. "Alexander F. Kerensky: The Political Career of a Russian Nationalist." Doctoral dissertation, Louisiana State University, Baton Rouge, 1976.

Kerensky, A. F. *The Kerensky Memoirs*. Cassell, London, 1966.

CHAPTER 8

On Brest-Litovsk

Felshtinsky, Yuri. *Lenin, Trotsky, Germany, and the Treaty of Brest-Litovsk*. Russell Enterprises, Milford, CT, 2012.

Kennan, George Frost. *Soviet Foreign Policy, 1917–1941*. Van Nostrand, Princeton, NJ, 1960.

Phillips, E. T. "Austria-Hungary and the Treaty of Brest-Litovsk." Master's thesis, Temple University, Philadelphia, 2012.

Robertson, P. W. "An Investigation of American Responses to the Russo-German Negotiations Resulting in the Treaty of Brest-Litovsk." Master's thesis, University of Wyoming, Laramie, 1964.

Trotsky, Leon. *From October to Brest-Litovsk*. Socialist Publication Society, New York, 1919.

Wargelin, Clifford Frank. "Bread, Peace and Poland: The Economic and Political Origins of Habsburg Policy at Brest-Litovsk." Doctoral dissertation, University of Wisconsin, Madison, 1980.

Wheeler-Bennett, John. *Brest-Litovsk: The Forgotten Peace*. Macmillan, London, 1938.

CHAPTER 9

Bailey, S. "Erich Ludendorff as Quartermaster General of the German Army, 1916–1918." Doctoral dissertation, University of Chicago, 1966.

Blaxland, Gregory. *Amiens, 1918*. Osprey, London, 2008.

Gray, Randall. *Kaiserschlacht, 1918: The Final German Offensive*. Osprey, London, 1991.

Hennes, Randolph York. "The March Retreat of 1918: Anatomy of a Battle." Doctoral dissertation, University of Washington, 1966.

Middlebrook, Martin. *The Kaiser's Battle*. Penguin, London, 2000.

Wilson, Dale Eldred. "'Treat 'em rough!': The United States Army Tank Corps in the First World War." Doctoral dissertation, Temple University, Philadelphia, 1990.

Zabecki, David T. *The German 1918 Offensives*. Routledge, New York, 2006.

CHAPTER 10

On Ludendorff's Collapse and the Blaming of the Jews

Chickering, R. *Imperial Germany and the Great War*. Cambridge University Press, Cambridge, 2004.

Diest, Wilhelm. "The Military Collapse of the German Empire: The Reality behind the Stab-in-the-Back Myth." *War in History* 3, no. 2 (1996):186–207.

Johnstone, Theodore A. "Dolchstoss: The Making of a Legend, 1890–1919." Doctoral dissertation, University of Kansas, Lawrence, 1974.

Romano, M. A. "The Stab in the Back Theory: From Myth to Genocide." Master's thesis, Kean University, Union, NJ, 2013.

Schvelbusch, Wolfgang. *The Culture of Defeat: On National Trauma, Mourning, and Recovery*. Picador Press, New York, 2004.

Scott, Allan C. "Dolchstosslegende and Jihad." Doctoral dissertation, Roosevelt University, Chicago, 2001.

Watson, Alexander. "Stabbed at the Front." *History Today* 58, no. 11 (November 2008):21–27.

CHAPTER 11

On Walter Rathenau

Felix, David. "Walter Rathenau and the Politics of Reparations." Doctoral dissertation, Columbia University, New York, 1970.

Kessler, Harry. *Walter Rathenau: His Life and Work*. Beston Press, New York, 1930.

Loewenberg, Peter Jacob. "Walter Rathenau and German Society." Doctoral dissertation, University of California, Berkeley, 1966.

Sanford, David George. "Walter Rathenau: Critic and Prophet of Imperial Germany." Doctoral dissertation, University of Michigan, Ann Arbor, 1971.

Smith, Gene Dixon. *The Ends of Greatness: Haig, Petain, Rathenau, and Eden*. Crown, New York, 1990.

Volkov, Shulamit. *Walter Rathenau*. Yale University Press, New Haven, CT, 2012.

Williamson, D. G. "Walter Rathenau: A Study of His Political, Industrial, and Cultural Activities." Doctoral dissertation, University of London, 1972.

On Ludendorff

Asprey, Robert. *The German High Command at War: Hindenburg and Ludendorff Conduct World War I.* W. Morrow, New York, 1991.

Bailey, Stephen. "Erich Ludendorff as Quartermaster General of the German Army, 1916–1918." Doctoral dissertation, University of Chicago, 1966.

Bridgman, John Marshall. "The Origins of the Military Dictatorship of Hindenburg and Ludendorff." Doctoral dissertation, Stanford University, 1960.

Bucelew, John Daniels. "Erich Ludendorff and the German War Effort: A Study in the Military Exercise of Power." Doctoral dissertation, University of California, San Diego, 1974.

Craven, Nancy Lynn. "Kuhlmann or Ludendorff." Doctoral dissertation, University of Chicago, 1969.

Lee, John. *The Warlords: Hindenburg and Ludendorff.* Weidenfeld & Nicolson, London, 2005.

Naftzger, Stephen Thomas. "Heil Ludendorff: Erich Ludendorff and Nazism, 1925–1937." Doctoral dissertation, City University of New York, 2002.

Nebelin, Manfred. *Ludendorff.* Siedleer Verlag, Munich, 2011.

Parkinson, Roger. *Tormented Warrior.* Stein & Day, New York, 1979.

Piazza, R. M. D. "Ludendorff: The Totalitarian and Voelkisch Politics of a Military Specialist." Doctoral dissertation, Northwestern University, Evanston, IL, 1969.

Wheeler-Bennett, John. *The Nemesis of Power: The German Army in Politics.* Macmillan Publishers, New York, 2005.

WORKS BY LUDENDORFF, WRITTEN AFTER THE DEFEATS OF 1918

Ludendorff, Erich. *The Nation at War.* Hutchinson and Company, London, 1936.

———. *The Defense of the Outpost Zone.* London, 1918.

———. *Ludendorff's Own Story*. Harper, New York, 1919.

———. *Lessons Drawn by the German Higher Command from the Recent Offensives*. General Staff Headquarters, London, 1918.

———. *The General Staff and Its Problems*. E. P. Dutton, New York, 1924.

———. *The Truth about Kitchener, to Which Is Appended a Letter from General von Ludendorff*. Bodley Head, London, 1925.

———. *The Two Battles of the Marne*. Cosmopolitan Book Corporation, New York, 1927.

———. "The American Soldier in the World War as Seen by a Foe." In *As They Saw Us*, edited by George Sylvester Viereck. Garden City, NY, 1929.

———. *The Coming War*. Faber & Faber, New York, 1931.

———. *Destruction of Freemasonry through Revelation of Its Secrets*. 1927. Sacred Truth Publishing House, 2014.

WORKS IN GERMAN OR FROM THE GERMAN

Anonymous. *Der Feldherr Ludendorff, Militarpolitisch betrachet von einem Soldaten*. Berlin, 1920.

Bauer, Max. *Der Grosse Krieg in Feld und Heimat*. Berlin, 1921.

Bethmann Hollweg, Theobald von. *Reflections on the World War*. T. Butterworth Publishers, London, 1920.

Breucker, Wilhelm. *Die Tragik Ludendorffs, Eine Kritische Studie*. Stollhamm, 1953.

Bruchmuller, Georg. *Die Artillerie beim Angriff im Stellungskrieg*. Berlin, 1926.

Conrad von Hötzendorf, Franz. *Aus Meiner Dienstzeit*, 1906–1918. Vienna, 1921.

Einem, Karl von. *Ein Armee Fuhrer erlebt den Weltkrieg*. Leipzig, 1938.

Foerster, Wolfgang. *Der Feldherr Ludendorff im Ungluck*. Weisbaden, 1932.

Frentz, Hans. *Der unbekannte Ludendorff, Der Feldherr in seiner Umwelt und Epoche.* Weisbaden, 1972.

Hindenburg, Paul von. *Out of My Life.* Harper, New York, 1921.

Hoffmann, Max. *War Diaries and Other Papers.* M. Secker, London, 1929.

———. *Tannenberg.* Berlin, 1925.

Hubatsch, W. *Hindenburg und der Staat.* Gottingen, 1966.

Janssen, Karl-Heinz. *Der Kanzler under dere General.* Gottingen, 1967.

Krebs, A. *Tendenzen und Geschichte der NSDAP.* Berlin, 1959.

Kuhl, H. von. *Der Weltkrieg 1914–1918.* Berlin, 1930.

Ludendorff, Erich. *Meine Kriegserinnerungen.* 2 vols. London, 1919.

Ludendorff, Margarethe. *My Married Life with Ludendorff.* Hutchinson, London, 1929.

Niemann, Alfred. *Kaiser und Revolution.* Berlin, 1922.

Ropponen, K. *Die Kraft Russlands.* Helsinki, 1968.

Rupprecht, crown prince of Bavaria. *Mein Kriegstagebuch.* Berlin, 1929.

Sulzbach, Herbert. *Zwei Lebende Mauern.* Berlin, 1935.

Tempelhof, Henny von. *Mein Gluck im Hause Ludendorff.* Berlin, 1918.

Tschuppik, Karl. *Ludendorff: The Tragedy of a Military Mind.* Houghton Mifflin, Boston, 1932.

Westarp, Kuno von. *Konservative Politick im letzten Jahrzelnt des Kaiserreichts,* vol. 2. Berlin, 1935.

Wheeler-Bennett, J. W. *Hindenburg: The Wooden Titan.* St. Martin's Press, New York, 1967.

Wilhelm, crown prince. *Memoirs.* Scribner's, New York, 1922.

Index